umber 44

Rossin, County Meath

An unofficial place

Bryn Coldrick

FOUR COURTS PRESS

Set in 10pt on 12pt Bembo by
Carrigboy Typesetting Services, County Cork for
FOUR COURTS PRESS LTD
Fumbally Lane, Dublin 8, Ireland
e-mail: info@four-courts-press.ie
http://www.four-courts-press.ie
and in North America for
FOUR COURTS PRESS
c/o ISBS, 5824 N.E. Hassalo Street, Portland, OR 97213.

ISBN 1-85182-710-2

Printed in Ireland by
ColourBooks Ltd, Dublin

Contents

Acknowledgements

My sincere thanks are due to many people for their advice, information, encouragement and guidance during my research.

To my thesis supervisor, Dr Colm Lennon for his kind words of encouragement and to Dr Raymond Gillespie, course leader, for his genuine enthusiasm and wide-ranging knowledge; and of course to all my colleagues on the MA Local History course 1998–2000. To the staffs of the National Archives; the National Library of Ireland; John Paul II Library, Maynooth; and the Public Record Office of Northern Ireland, who all provided access to their valuable collections of material. Special thanks are due to Andrew Bennett and to all the staff of Meath County Library, Navan. Also to Paul Ferguson, map librarian, Trinity College Dublin.

To the locals of Rossin, who played such an important role in the gathering of ideas and information, and for the inspiration which came from their palpable community spirit. Although my thanks go to all Rossin's residents, special mention should be made of the following individuals: Frank Taaffe, Liam Taaffe, Mary Taaffe, Jack Cole, Assumpta Smith, Teresa Martin, James Martin, Helen-Anne Tully, Claire Mullen, Ollie Grimes and the late Mary-Alice Smith.

To Geraldine Stout, whose in-depth knowledge of the history of the area, acquired through many years of tireless research, proved a source of information and inspiration. She should especially be acknowledged for bringing the Campbell-Hall lease and the Bernard Scalé map to my attention. To Grant Hill for his architectural knowledge and editorial comments; to my parents, William and Linda Coldrick, and to Judy Hill, for their on-going interest in the research.

Finally and most sincerely, I would like to thank my partner, Karina Hill, for her continued support and encouragement, and, not least, for her computer skills and forbearance which proved invaluable in the face of the occasional emergency.

Introduction

Rossin is not a town, a parish or a townland. The placename is an unofficial one describing an abstract entity, the boundaries of which are indefinable. The area known as Rossin overlaps the boundaries of three official townlands (Monknewtown, Balfaddock and Dowth) and two parishes (Monknewtown and Dowth) on the eastern extremity of Co. Meath at the border with Co. Louth. Today, Rossin is conspicuous on the N51 midway between Slane and Drogheda because, in an otherwise agricultural landscape of open fields and sparsely located houses, there suddenly appears a small shop ('Smiths'), a recently re-thatched and renovated public house ('The tourists rest' or 'Mitchells'), a Roman Catholic chapel, a school house, the ruins of a medieval church with graveyard and, most strikingly of all, the magnificent remains of a ruined Georgian mill. Between these are a small number of dwellings, some with nineteenth-century elements and one derelict building with an eighteenth-century outward appearance. The sites of many more dwellings have been cleared. All this is located within a radius of a hundred yards or so just before a triple-arched humpback bridge carries the main road over the River Mattock into Louth and on towards Drogheda via King William's Glen and the battle of the Boyne site (fig. 1).

Proto-villages of this kind are dotted all around Ireland and many (especially in Leinster) are the remnants of Anglo-Norman boroughs like Colp near Drogheda or even Dowth near Rossin itself. Rossin does indeed have some of the hallmarks of a medieval settlement, the most obvious being its ruined church. There is no record of a castle in Rossin, however, which no medieval manor or borough could exist without. The most significant argument against Rossin's origins relating to Anglo-Norman settlement are toponymical. The name Rossin is applied to the small area only by the locals themselves and has never been recognized as an official placename by local administration or by central government. Colp, Dowth and all other medieval settlements are not only recognized in official records, they usually gave their names to the surrounding parish. If Rossin had existed in medieval times, therefore, there would almost certainly be a Rossin parish or townland and the place would be represented in the historical documents. The origin of Rossin as a name and a settlement, therefore, is something of a mystery, a mystery which this essay attempts to tackle.

To the people initially interviewed, among them locals whose families have lived in Rossin for generations, the name and by association the settlement itself, owes its existence to the community's most eye-catching structure: the

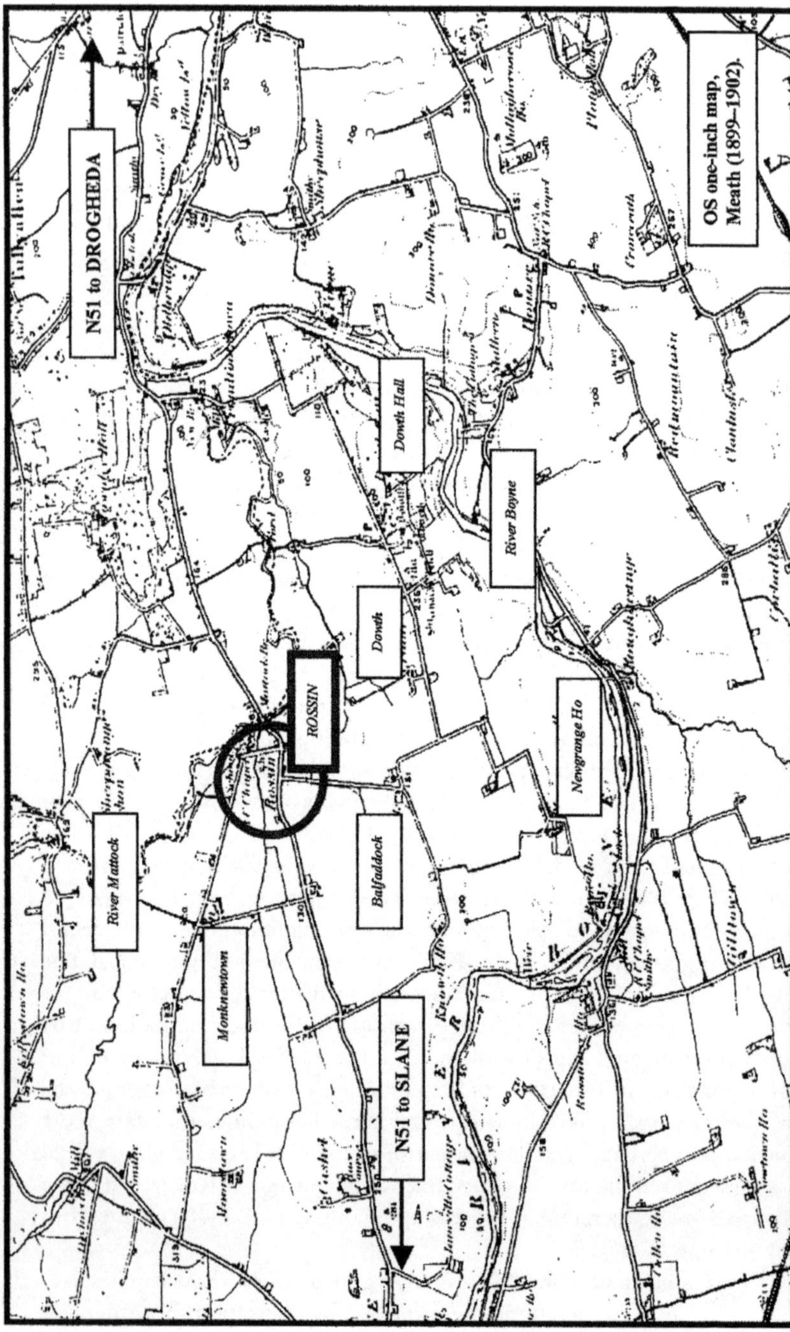

1 Location map, based on one-inch OS map (1899–1902).

ruined mill. According to local tradition, Rossin Mill took its name from a man associated with the enterprise and the area immediately around it, in turn, took its name from the mill. The children of the 1930s, and presumably their parents and grandparents who passed on the stories to them, could not remember whether Rossin was the mill's owner or 'the wicked caretaker who lived in the millyard and would not let the people go to mass'.[1] It is tempting to accept the theory that the community of Rossin could have been born out of the grinding mill stones in what has been regarded as an eighteenth-century flour mill. Perhaps a micro-industrial revolution took place here, attracting workers from the surrounding district and giving a milling livelihood to dozens of households. Although the mill has long been a majestic ruin, the descendants of these millers continue to drink in the pub, buy their milk in the shop, worship in the chapel and turn out to support Rossin Rovers, the local soccer team, on cold and wet Sunday mornings.

This creation myth continues to be related by the community for want of an alternative but when one looks more closely, however, the story becomes less straightforward. Indeed, just two documents are sufficient to reveal that Rossin Mill could not have created Rossin the community because the name, and therefore the community, existed more than one hundred years prior to the building of the mill. The mill, therefore, was not the genesis of Rossin; it was merely one stage in its overall development.

In order to address the origins of Rossin and to understand it in the context of a tradition of settlement in the area, we have to try to trace the wider developments in the locality stretching back long before the establishment of the mill itself. In many ways, this is a tale of two parishes – Monknewtown and Dowth – meeting each other on the Slane–Drogheda road. It is also the tale of three townlands – Monknewtown, Dowth and the much smaller Balfaddock (fig. 2). It is the developments within and relationships between these official units that we must examine. What we will see when considering the two larger townlands is a shift of focus – economic, social, spiritual – from one to the other, and a convergence of settlement on the western side of the Mattock River where the three townlands meet. Most importantly, it becomes increasingly clear that Rossin as a community is just one expression of a tradition of small-scale localized settlement in the bend of the Boyne that began with the first people to populate the area in prehistory. And just like its predecessors and counterparts, the community of Rossin was brought about and was at all times influenced by external forces in the form of local geography, particular personalities or 'brokers', and the wider social, political and economic forces which existed all around it.

One of the most crucial aspects of the character of Rossin is its sense of identity beyond the townland level. The limitations of undertaking a local history which aims to tell the story of a rural community based on the townland or parish unit have already been accepted by those practising the discipline in Ireland today. Rather than an artificial creation of political or religious administration, Rossin developed as a group of people living in close proximity to one another and was bound as a community by kinship, work, place and play. Publicly-available sources lend themselves easily to townland and parish histories but a townland or parish history of Monknewtown, Balfaddock or Dowth could completely overlook the very existence of Rossin or, at best, refer to it in a brief aside. This short book attempts to trace the origin, growth and decline of Rossin as an actual community that spilled across three official townlands and to put that community into some form of historical context. But the fact that it is an unofficial place and placename means that Rossin is almost completely invisible in the historical documents. This inevitably makes it extremely difficult to locate material which would help to tell the story of the local community in particular and although the focus is kept on Rossin as much as possible, the absence of publicly-available source material dealing directly with Rossin itself makes it necessary to infer much about the nature and experience of the community by way of reference to its immediate environment. Whether this book is successful in telling the story of a community distinct from the townlands in which it was located, or whether it is a lesson in the limitations of using publicly-available material to achieve such aims, is for the reader to decide.

The first chapter sets the scene for the future Rossin community by examining briefly in turn each of the official entities that Rossin occupies. It discusses the qualities of the local landscape which attracted the first settlers to the area and the impact they had on that landscape. The chapter moves on to trace the land divisions as imposed by successive peoples from the Gaels and the Cistercian monks to the Anglo-Norman settlers and looks at the similarities, differences and relationships between each of these official places. The purpose of the chapter is to provide an historical background of Rossin prior to the emergence of the community so that it can be understood in terms of an ancient tradition of shifting settlement patterns in the area.

The second chapter considers the emergence of Rossin into this ancient landscape and begins by attempting to answer the biggest question of all – when did this unofficial place emerge and how? Although the mystery remains to some extent unsolved, local tradition is challenged by recorded history and it seems increasingly likely that although Rossin had been recognised as a place decades earlier, the settlement itself developed as part of the reorganization of the local landed estates in the second half of the eighteenth century. The chapter follows in some detail the process of estate reorganization which was anything but a smooth one and introduces the people and the factors that played a part in the evolving community which expressed itself through the various facilities that made Rossin more than a typical rural settlement. Not least, this chapter describes the background to the establishment of Rossin Mill, previously considered to be the genesis of

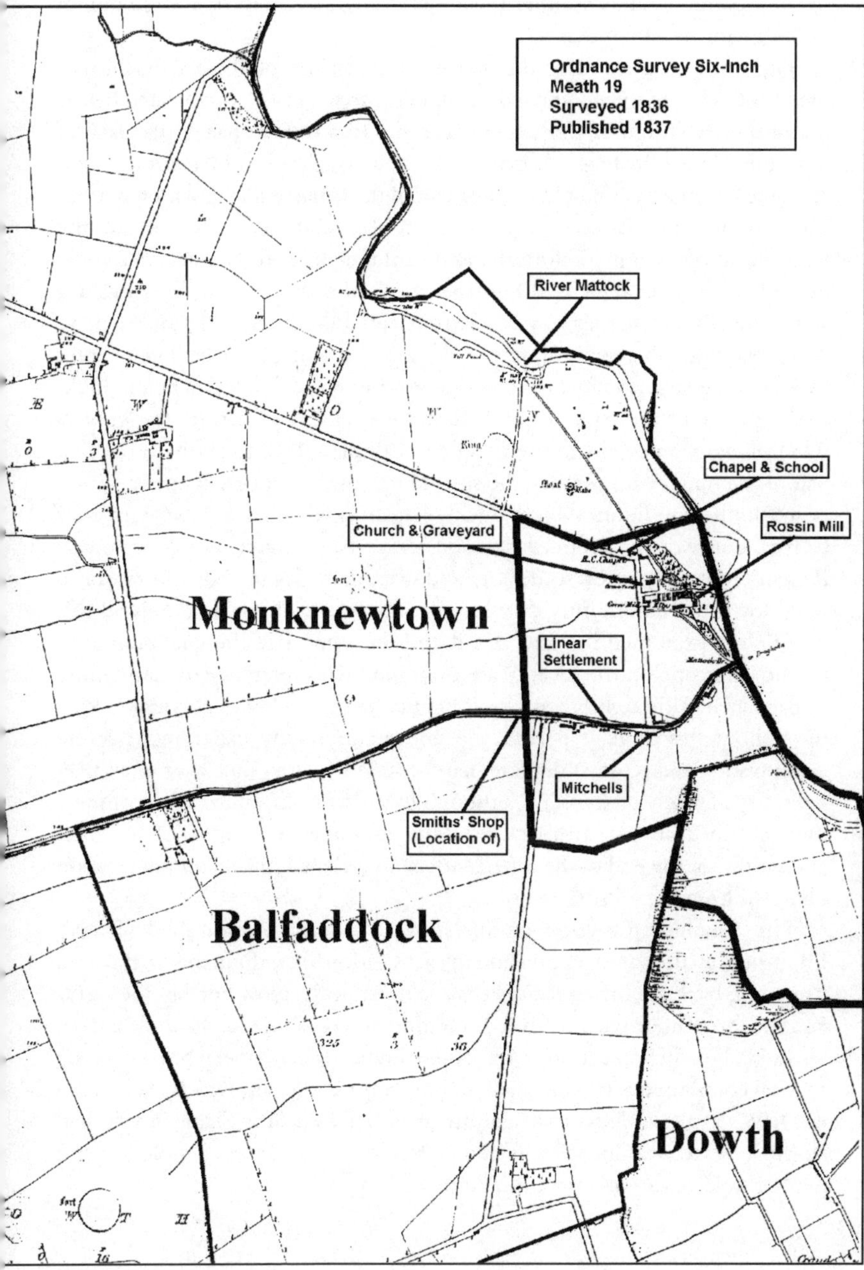

2 Detailed Rossin area map, based on first edition OS map (1837).

the community and its unofficial name but now known to have been one of its last major developments.

The third chapter traces the growth and decline of Rossin during the nineteenth century when initial developments were at first consolidated before the overall evolution of the settlement came to a sudden halt in the face of unfavourable external circumstances. The new mill, we can be confident, was enjoying booming business in the first half of the century, like its counterpart in Slane. Community facilities which were in place and serving Rossin and the wider local community before the end of the eighteenth century, were now upgraded. The overall focus of human settlement and activity in the rural area was gradually gravitating towards Rossin and Rossin itself appears to have developed into what could almost be described as a small village. The chapter examines the factors that contributed to this period of development and looks at the nature of the community that was evolving. But despite the growth which Rossin enjoyed and the potential it displayed, particularly in the first half of the nineteenth century, the second half of the century brought with it post-Famine conditions which quickly began to take their toll. A number of factors, not least the reduced demand for cereal produce, not only caused Rossin's milling business to decline and eventually dry up, but also began to drag down the community of which it was a part. The factors behind this decline are examined in some detail and the impact of the changing economic landscape on the locality are examined with reference to land tenure in particular. Although Rossin itself maintained a steady net population level throughout this difficult period, the wider community experienced severe depopulation and Rossin's development became frozen in time after more than a century of steady progress. Yet, although its growth was stunted, the community remained alive and this chapter also examines the nature of the local community at the end of the nineteenth century, based mainly on information obtained from the 1901 Census.

The concluding section of this study is subtitled 'unfinished village'. Emerging as the latest expression of a tradition of settlement in the area stretching back centuries, factors on a national level, most notably the Great Famine, prevented Rossin from becoming an actual village in the modern sense. Had the depopulation of the post-Famine years not been so devastating to local communities in general, there is no apparent reason why Rossin could not have developed into a village similar in size to nearby Slane. Rossin had all the necessary facilities for its people but in the end it was people it could neither hold onto nor attract in a sustainable way.

I. Official places: the bend of the Boyne since prehistory

As early as 4000 BC, in a period known to archaeologists as the Neolithic, it became apparent that Ireland's central plain, of which the future county of Meath would form a part, was amongst the most fertile areas on the entire island. As the primeval forests were cut back to reveal the land's enormous potential for yielding rich cereal crops and supporting successful herds of livestock, this area became one of the most coveted parts of the country. This was true not just to these first farmers but to the successive generations of settlers throughout the millennia that were to follow and the fertility of the land, with careful nurturing, would play a central role in the lives of all those who would live there until very recently.[1]

The agricultural and economic importance of the Boyne valley, coupled with the particular topography and strategic location of the bend of the Boyne, helped to make this the ritual centre of Neolithic Ireland. A lasting monument to the special regard with which the bend of the Boyne was held by the society of that time exists today as the Brú na Bóinne archaeological complex, a UNESCO world heritage site. This complex, which includes the area occupied by Rossin (i.e. the townlands of Monknewtown, Balfaddock and Dowth) as well as neighbouring Newgrange and Knowth, contains some of the most important Neolithic passage tombs in western Europe. The cemetery as a whole comprises around forty of these monuments ranging in date from *c.*3200 BC to *c.*3000 BC. The impact which the Neolithic people left on the landscape of the Rossin area would continue to be felt in subsequent periods of the area's history.

The continued spiritual and mystical importance of the bend of the Boyne to Ireland's inhabitants is indicated by the special place it occupies in Celtic folklore with Newgrange being regarded, among other things, as a gateway to the underworld to which the Tuatha de Danann retreated with the arrival of the Celts. Tourists from Roman Britain would have passed through the Rossin area to visit the *brú* or palace of Aengus (Newgrange) and to leave offerings of coins and jewellery at the entrance to the great mound. The Celtic kings of North Brega would use the Neolithic cemetery at Knowth, also only a stone's throw from modern Rossin, as a fortress capital with a substantial Early Christian settlement located in and around the tombs. During medieval times, the tumuli of Knowth and Dowth would both be adapted by the Anglo-Normans as convenient readymade mottes which could be fortified without having to go to the expense of creating an artificial mound as was necessary elsewhere. After the initial invasion, the great tomb of Knowth would become the centre of a monastic grange while Dowth would become the location for a medieval manorial village which was framed by the tumulus on one side and a tower house on the other. Even if they were sometimes simply regarded as a convenient quarry for building material or a convenient ready-made mound, the passage graves of the bend of the Boyne were an integral part of the local landscape and would certainly have contributed to Rossin's sense of place as they still do today.

The division of Ireland into townlands, parishes, counties, and provinces has a long history and it is necessary to trace these ever-shifting political and ecclesiastical divisions in order to place the future community of Rossin into an historical and local political context. During the first century AD, Ireland was divided into five ancient kingdoms known as 'the five fifths of Ireland' and the future Rossin was located in North Leinster, the capital of which was the Hill of Tara. By the end of the first century, the people of Conn had crossed the Shannon and had begun to annex lands around present-day Mullingar. Thus, the new kingdom of Meath ('the middle kingdom') was born with its initial capital at Uisneach. By the third century, Tara, which had a similar mystical status to the bend of the Boyne, had been adopted as the capital of the new kingdom of Meath. By the sixth century, resistance to Meath's supremacy in Leinster had evaporated and Meath had been divided into 17 subkingdoms with the future Rossin area being included in North Brega and located less than a mile from its capital Cnogbha or Knowth.[2]

This situation remained unchanged throughout the Early Christian period until the coming of the Anglo-Normans in 1169. Soon after this event, a new administrative division was introduced: the parish system which was adopted following the synod of Cashel in 1171–2 as part of a series of reforms designed to reorganise a church in disarray. Dowth (known to the Celts as Dubhadh or 'darkness' as a result of the tomb's unsavoury creation myth) became a parish under this system and the ruined church which exists today dates to this time. Monknewtown also became a parish and Rossin would later emerge between them. One lasting effect the parish system had on the character of the local area was the foundation of new stone churches which in many cases, including Dowth, became the focus for medieval manorial communities.

Prior to this, the landscape of the bend of the Boyne, north and south of the river, had begun a second agricultural revolution with the arrival in 1142 of the Cistercian monks who established their first Irish house at nearby Mellifont. The style of land management which they exercised over the huge tracts of farmland granted to them by the local Gaelic king represented the most revolutionary landscape change the Boyne valley had seen since the forests had been cleared in the early Neolithic period. By 1539, Mellifont Abbey held up to 11,000 acres including estates and rights over much of the

Boyne valley.[3] Mellifont had divided this land into independent monastic farms or 'granges' which were managed by teams of lay brethren. The granges under the control of Mellifont included Newgrange, Knowth, Balfaddock, Monknewtown and many more townlands throughout the locality. The grange began as a small group of farm buildings but, in most cases, eventually developed into a small nucleated settlement (similar to the manorial villages of the Anglo-Normans) with Monknewtown being a good example of this evolutionary process.[4]

The name Monknewtown derives from Baile nua na Manach, literally 'the monks' new town'. The ruins of the medieval church and graveyard remain nestled between the shell of Rossin Mill and the nineteenth-century chapel and it seems certain that this area was the location for one of the many granges in the locality. Many of these granges contained corn mills and although there is a possibility that Monknewtown was no exception, there is no record of one here. In 1348, the place known as the New Town de Munkland was confirmed to the abbey by King Edward III along with the townland of Ballyfeddock and others.[5] The original grant was made long before this in the reign of Edward's great-grandfather, Henry III, who ruled from 1216 to 1272.[6] Around 1403, Pope Boniface IX issued a papal bull to the monastery of Mellifont confirming that the monastery with all its chapels, granges (including Monknewtown) and people, were exempt from the jurisdiction of ordinary judges as it had been 'since time immorial'. The bull was issued at the request of the abbot of Mellifont to prove his case against the bishop of Meath who was, at the time, attempting to claim subsidies from the churches within the lordship of the abbey.[7]

The Cistercian granges of the Boyne valley became the facilitators of a kind of agriculture of such efficiency and intensity that it has been compared to the industrial agricultural practices which are carried on by some of the farms in the area today. Grain cultivation, cattle breeding and sheep rearing were conducted extensively in the Boyne valley under the patronage of the Cistercians. In the thirteenth century, grain from here was being exported to England while archaeological evidence in Balfaddock and Knowth indicates intensive ploughing of the soil. In addition to increasing the intensity of the agriculture practised in the Boyne valley, the Cistercians also revolutionised its milling and fishing industries. Twelfth-century documents make numerous references to the fishing weirs, mills and millponds of the Boyne and by the time the monastery was dissolved in 1539, the Cistercians were still operating several flour mills including one at Newgrange known as 'Broe's Mill' and fishing weirs including one at Knowth.[8]

Although the bend of the Boyne was clearly dominated by its religious landowners, the Anglo-Norman invasion of 1169–70 reintroduced secular settlement to the area, in particular at Dowth. Having been granted the liberty of Meath by Henry II in 1172, Hugh de Lacy subdivided it into smaller areas which he granted to subtenants in a process known as subinfeudation. His grantees, in turn, subdivided their holdings into manors of which Dowth was one. Upon receipt of a land grant, it was the responsibility of the grantee to ensure that his holding was adequately defended with fortifications such as a motte-and-bailey castle. It is believed that the tumuli at Dowth and Knowth were both utilised for this purpose by Netterville and Richard le Fleming of Slane respectively. The next step was to encourage immigrants to leave their homes in England and Wales and make the journey to Ireland, settling and farming the land in order to make the manor an economically viable unit in the same way that the lay brethren were doing for the nearby Cistercian abbey through the granges.[9]

It should be remembered that, at the time, the Irish landscape was almost exclusively open farmland and forests with the only urban centres being the Norse walled towns of Dublin, Limerick and a few others. The only pre-Norman settlements of note in Meath were the ancient monastic foundations such as Kells, Slane, Duleek, Skreen and Clonard.[10] The native Irish were still mainly living in ringforts dispersed across the landscape. A ringfort is a small farmstead which appears today as a small circular enclosure formed by a low bank of earth and stones often with a ditch outside the bank. Antiquarians of the nineteenth century believed that these were military forts built by the Danes but it is now accepted by archaeologists that they were simply farmsteads or enclosures for livestock built and used mainly during the Early Christian period (from around 400 to around 1150). Ringforts are the most common type of archaeological monument in the country and any place-name in use today containing the element 'rath', 'dun', 'lis', or 'cashel' owes its origins to one of these ancient farmsteads.

The primary form of settlement in medieval Meath was the manorial village. Generally, this comprised a castle (a motte-and-bailey and later a stone tower house), a manorial church (which could either pre-date or post-date the castle), and a number of dwellings. A total of ninety-eight manorial villages from this period had been identified in Meath by 1974. The majority of these became abandoned from around the seventeenth century onwards and in most cases the only upstanding indications of the village site today are the more endurable remnants such as the castle or church. Dwellings constructed of mud and wattle have long since disappeared leaving little or no visible trace above ground level. Earthworks have been known to preserve the line of former streets or property boundaries but in the majority of cases, these too have been ploughed out by centuries of intensive agriculture.[11]

At the height of their power in the first half of the thirteenth century, the Anglo-Norman conquerors held no more than two-thirds of the country. During the fourteenth and fifteenth centuries, their authority was in continuous decline until they effectively controlled only the area occupied by the modern counties of Dublin, Louth, Meath and Kildare. In 1495, this area was designated 'The Pale' under an act of parliament and it became the area in which English dress, customs, language and political power flourished most in opposition to the native culture all around it. In terms of agriculture and settlement patterns, the impact of the Anglo-Normans within the Pale was revolutionary and apart from Dublin, Meath became the most intensively settled part of Ireland.[12]

The Civil Survey of 1654–6 recorded 170 tower houses in Meath but by the time of the 1884 edition of the Ordnance Survey maps for the county, that number had fallen to only seventy-two upstanding remains or known sites. Most of the tower houses in the county date to the fifteenth century and were almost exclusively built on high ground near to a river for strategic and transport reasons. The tower house was the focal point of the lordship, representing a source of employment and protection for the local peasant community. When a tower house was under construction, all men within the lordship were obliged under a statute of 1431 to work eight days of the year for three years on the castle and thereafter, their economic lives would centre around the castle economy.[13] Dowth Castle would have acted as a focus in this way.

By the time of the dissolution of the monasteries from 1539 onwards, when monastic land was forfeited to the crown and redistributed to loyal crown subjects, Mellifont held not only Monknewtown and Balfaddock but also the neighbouring townlands of Newgrange, Knowth and Kellystown and the nearby townlands of Tullyallen, Sheepgrange, Littlegrange, Collon, and Oldbridge. What we have in the bend of the Boyne, therefore, is a landscape primarily occupied by monastic farmland and granges with a small number of secular settlements dispersed over the area. Focussing on the site of the future Rossin community, we have a later monastic grange almost at the location of Rossin itself with the secular manor and townland of Dowth bordering it to the south.

A grant from King James I in 1612 bestowed Munke Newtowne (also known as 'the town, village and hamlet of Rathmiskin') on Sir Garret Moore of Mellifont. The Moore family would later become earls of Drogheda and the ultimate landlords for the southern half of Rossin in the eighteenth century. At the time of their initial grant in 1612, Monknewtown contained seven messuages (stone houses) and 10 cottages with 168 acres of arable land, 40 acres of pasture, eight acres of meadow as well as furze and briars.[14] No mention was made of a mill, however, which suggests that if a medieval mill had ever existed in Monknewtown in association with the grange, it was gone even before the 1540s. The Civil Survey, which was a 'Domesday Book' for the southern and eastern parts of Ireland compiled in 1654–6 to aid the transfer of land from Catholic 'rebels' to Protestant British 'adventurers' and soldiers, tells us that in 1640 the parish of Monknewtown contained 590 acres and that 500 of these was used for arable farming. This left 40 acres as meadow and pasture with the remaining 50 acres under forest. It was still owned by the Moore family, specifically Sir Gerald Moore of Mellifont who owned all of that lordship and other lands in the region. There was still no mention of a mill.[15]

The second parish of which Rossin forms a part is Dowth. As we have seen, the townland of Dowth represented a secular island in a monastic sea in medieval times. The first castle here is said to have been erected by de Lacy who granted the manor to the Nettervilles.[16] The Netterville family originated in Nutrevilla, a small town in France, and the most renowned member of the family was Luke Netterville who became archbishop of Armagh in 1216 and established the Dominican friary in Drogheda (the Magdalene tower being the last upstanding remnant).[17] The manor of Dowth in the mid-thirteenth century covered an area of 1,463 acres or five ploughlands. There were three Irish and three English fee-paying tenants; one English and one Irish 'free tenant'; and a few cottiers. Dowth Castle, which remains to this day, is a fifteenth-century tower house surrounded by a medieval field system between the church and the Neolithic tumulus.[18] With the suppression of the monasteries in the middle of the sixteenth century, the rectory and tithes of Dowth passed to Sir Gerald Moore and not to the traditional Catholic landowners of Dowth, the Nettervilles. In December 1569, Queen Elizabeth I confirmed to Edward Moore the parsonage and tithes of Dowth in the towns and hamlets of Dowth and Proudfootstown.[19] The Nettervilles, however, held on to the estate of Dowth despite the uncertainty of their position through much of the seventeenth century and remained a very wealthy and important family into the nineteenth.

In 1640, Dowth townland comprised one and a half ploughlands or 442 acres (340 acres arable; sixty pasture; thirty meadow and twelve acres of bogland). The manor of Dowth comprised the castle, a stone house, a stable and other outhouses. There was also a church, a farm house, a malthouse and bawn, a corn mill, a tuck mill, a salmon weir and a pigeon house.[20] So medieval and even early modern Dowth was a hive of human activity, much more so than Monknewtown and something which would change by the early eighteenth century. The decline of Dowth may have taken place during a long period unrest which began in 1641 with the destruction of the church which was dedicated to St Sinnac.[21]

Although Dowth townland took up most of Dowth parish, there were other entities within it. For instance, there was the now-abandoned village of Craud and the townland of Proudfootstown. Proudfootstown seems to have come into being in the fifteenth century and an indenture reproduced in the Drogheda Papers records that during the reign of Edward IV, probably in 1461, an agreement was made between the abbot of Mellifont on the one part and Richard Proudfoot of Proudfootstown, gentleman, and Patrick, his son and heir on the other. A dispute had arisen over some land which the Proodfoots had taken as their own, much to the anger of the abbot. The indenture sought to remedy the dispute by formally defining the boundaries of Proudfootstown.[22] The Civil Survey recorded that Proudfootstown contained a castle, a stone house, an orchard, and a corn mill, all of which by then belonged to Sir Gerald Moore of Mellifont, as well as a quarter of a ploughland or 130 acres (100 arable, 10 meadow and 20 pasture) which was shared by two men – Moore and Netterville who held one moiety each.

Compared to the description of Monknewtown parish in the same source, it seems that Dowth parish in 1641 contained the foci of human activity, specifically in Dowth Manor, Proudfootstown and Craud. By the late eighteenth century, however, Dowth was almost entirely made up of farms and farmland. There were still two small mills but nothing else which would indicate a concentration of settlement such as a place of worship or a school, remained. It was still very much alive agriculturally of course but the outlets of extra-agricultural activity had shifted to Rossin on the border with the neighbouring townland of Monknewtown by the latter decades of the eighteenth century.

The final townland which Rossin covers is that of Balfaddock, also in the parish of Monknewtown. The centre of modern-day Rossin is located in Balfaddock and contains the public house and the shop. This townland is situated in the eastern part of the parish and the name means 'the town of the plovers'.[23] Balfaddock was also confirmed to Mellifont Abbey by Edward III and after the dissolution it was granted to Sir Garret Moore. At the time, it contained seven messuages, one cottage and land divided into 227 acres arable and five acres meadow.[24] By the end of the eighteenth century, its main landlord was Andrew Caldwell of Newgrange and it contained just over 325 acres, all of which was cultivated at the time apart from a small area of marsh.

The present landscape of Co. Meath owes its origins to the nature of late seventeenth and eighteenth-century landholding arrangements and agricultural practices.[25] The medieval villages were gradually deserted as people gravitated towards the towns and pastureland gradually increased (especially in the second half of the nineteenth century), replacing the medieval agricultural economy. One of the most decisive factors in the nature of the local landscape was the battle of the Boyne, fought between William of Orange and James II on 1 July 1690 all around the Rossin area. The battle ended James's hopes of regaining the crown from his Protestant son-in-law and the war finally ended on 3 October 1691 with the signing of the treaty of Limerick. This paved the way for the confiscation and resettlement of land, the introduction of the Penal Laws, and for two hundred years of Protestant Ascendancy. History would prove it to be one of the most important and controversial battles in Irish history.

The landscape changes that had begun in the aftermath of the dissolution of the monasteries were consolidated by the Williamite land settlement. The gradual enclosure of monastic grange lands after 1539 was formalized during the eighteenth century by regular hedgerows which divided the land into farms of various sizes. The eighteenth century also witnessed tremendous advances and improvements in land management and agricultural practices. Farms were leased to tenants who often sublet their holdings to subtenants which created a pyramid in which local farmers spanned almost the entire range of the social spectrum from the numerically-superior small cottiers with their mud-walled houses, through the middle and strong farmers with their more comfortable and more durable stone houses, to a handful of major, usually Protestant, landlords whose dwellings reflected their social, political and economic standing.[26]

The constituent townlands and parishes of Rossin had different backgrounds, different landlords and different experiences, all of which would contribute in some way to the character of Rossin and its people. Monknewtown and Balfaddock had been monastic lands until the 1540s when they were forfeited from Mellifont Abbey and granted to Sir Gerald Moore. Balfaddock became the property of Charles Campbell and then Charles and Andrew Caldwell of Newgrange while Monknewtown would pass to the earl of Sheffield. Dowth largely remained the property of the Nettervilles since the time of the Anglo-Norman invasion in the twelfth century and remained a centre of human activity until the seventeenth century.) Towards the end of the following century, however, a shift in focus had taken place which saw Dowth become almost entirely a townland of farms and fields while Monknewtown experienced large-scale improvements. Rossin, where the three townlands met, became the venue for much of the development of Monknewtown and Balfaddock. The next chapter examines the effects of eighteenth-century estate management on the Rossin area and suggests that the reorganization of the estates may even be the first steps in the creation of the Rossin community itself.

2. The emergence of Rossin: 1724–1825

Rossin has never before been the subject of published study, due in part perhaps to the fact that its very nature as an unofficial place has meant that historical documents, in particular official records, have almost completely overlooked its very existence. Rossin has been invisible in the writings of most local historians and secondary sources make only passing references to one aspect of the community, the mill.[1] The enduring tradition in the area is that the unofficial placename of Rossin owes it existence to the mill. The most popular theory is that Mr Rossin was the mill owner or the man who built it and one little girl was told by her grandmother as recently as 1938, in what may be interpreted as collective memory of Penal times, that Rossin was the wicked caretaker who would not let the local people go to mass.[2] The local historian's task seems simple then – date the mill and you date the community.

Rossin Mill (also referred to as Monknewtown Mill) has been described as an eighteenth-century structure, presumably in light of its overtly Georgian appearance (fig. 3). It has also been dated to 1809–10 by Conlon and others, probably because of a letter in the Sheffield Papers in which the owner of the estate, John Baker Holroyd, earl of Sheffield, comments on the proposals of a Mr Rodgers to build a mill in Monknewtown.[3] Although Rodgers did indeed become the mill's operator shortly after its completion, he did not actually build it himself as another document in the Sheffield Papers shows. The document in question is a lease, dated 22 October 1825, made between the Right Hon. George Augustus Frederick Charles Holroyd, earl of Sheffield, and Townley Blackwood Hardman Esq. who came from a wealthy farming family in the vicinity of Drogheda. The lease was made for three lives renewable forever of part of the lands of Monknewtown, Co. Meath, 'for the purpose of erecting a mill thereon':

> … And whereas the said Townley Blackwood Hardman hath applied to the said Earl of Sheffield to grant unto him a lease for lives renewable forever of part of the said lands of Monknewtown containing three acres plantation measure and which is not any part of the demesne usually occupied by the said Earl of Sheffield with his Mansion House for the purpose of building and erecting a corn mill thereon with the necessary mill pond and mill dam for the same at the yearly rent of five pounds per acre and a renewable fine of seven pounds ten shillings on the fall of each life being one half of the years rent agreed … the said

3 Rossin Mill (July 2000).

> Townley Blackwood Hardman agreed to erect and make at his own expense within the period of two years … [a mill] for the purpose of grinding and preparing corn and flour and a mill pond or mill dam for same …[4]

This lease demonstrates beyond a reasonable doubt that the mill in Rossin cannot predate 1825, a fact which is also supported by other written and cartographic sources. Taking folk memory at face value, therefore, would date the community of Rossin to sometime after 1825. Unfortunately for folk memory, on this occasion the facts do not support tradition. The mill, as we now know, could not have been built before 1825 but the grand jury presentment books record sums of money allocated towards filling ditches along the Slane to Drogheda road as far as 'Rossin' in 1813. Furthermore, the Catholic parish registers for Grangegeeth Union record almost 80 baptisms of children born in 'Rossin' between 1785 and 1815. These children were born to parents who identified with the community of Rossin and not, as almost every other entry shows, with an official townland. The register also records the marriage of two Rossin couples in 1787. Ten years earlier, in 1777, Thomas Reynolds from that part of Rossin bordering the north side of the Slane–Drogheda road opposite Mitchells' public house was buried in Monknewtown churchyard and was described on his headstone as a 'Rosson' man.

Undoubtedly, the most important original document available during the research and one which confirms that the name, and therefore the community, was in existence as much as a century before the mill, is a memorial of a lease agreement made between Charles Campbell of Newgrange and Edward Hall of 'Rossen' which was signed on 2 November 1724.[5] This is the earliest known reference to Rossin of which this writer is currently aware and is transcribed below:

> A memorial of a lease bearing date the twenty ninth day of August one thousand seven hundred and twenty four made between Charles Campbell of Newgrange in the county of Meath Esq. of the one part and Edward Hall of Rossen in the said county of Meath Farmer of the other part, whereby the said Charles Campbell for the considerations therein mentioned did demise grant sell and to farm lett unto the said Edward Hall all that part or parcell of the town and lands of Balfaddock containing twenty acres plantation measure be[ing] the same more or less than in his possession lying upon the south side of the highway leading from Mattock Bridge to Slane partly enclosed with a new ditch adjoining to the ditch on the highway with the rector[y]. All tythes yearly coming growing arising and renewing in the said twenty acres situated in the Barony of Slane and county of Meath with the appurtances except as in the said lease is excepted to hold to the said Edward Hall his [executors] [administrators] and assigns from the first day of May past for the term of thirty one years at and under the rent of eight pounds ten shillings sterling payable half yearly above all taxes. [To] which said lease and this memorial are witnessed by the Revd. Peter Jackson of Killincool in the county of Lowth [clerk] and William Colvill of the City of Dublin Gent. [clerk] to the said Charles Campbell etc.[6]

The location of Hall's holding described above is depicted cartographically in 1766 on an estate map produced by Bernard Scalé for Charles Caldwell who was Campbell's successor in Newgrange.[7] On this invaluable map, the holding occupied by Edward Hall's descendant and successor, Luke Hall, corresponds in terms of today's Rossin with the location of Smiths' shop and the land which extends from there to the south and west (fig. 4).

In light of the information contained in the two documents cited above, it now seems clear that Rossin Mill was more than likely built by Townley Blackwood Hardman between 1825 and 1827, at least 100 years after the placename of Rossin had entered common usage in the area and at least 100 years after the emergence of the community. It also seems unlikely that the name refers to an individual as local tradition supposes though we should not be too quick to dismiss folk memory on the matter as in this area folk memory has a proven track record. From the last prehistoric occurrence of the

4 Caldwell estate map by Bernard Scalé, 1766.

winter solstice phenomenon at Newgrange towards the end of the Neolithic period until Professor Michael J. O'Kelly unblocked the roof box to become the first modern human being to witness the event in 1967, the locals had preserved the memory of the fact that the sun entered the tomb. This is an almost incredible example of folk memory preserving local information from the Stone Age, passing it down from one generation to the next through fireside stories. If the people of the bend of the Boyne were able to remember this phenomenon for over four and a half thousand years, perhaps there is some element of truth to the accepted belief that the name and the emergence of Rossin is somehow linked to a mill. If folk memory is indeed mistaken, as the documents suggest, it is unlikely to matter much to the community anyway.

Although Rossin is certainly not associated with the present mill, there remains a possibility that a former mill operated in Monknewtown before the coming of the present structure in the 1820s. As discussed in more detail in the first chapter, this was the monks' new town, a grange settlement under the jurisdiction of Mellifont Abbey with a medieval church whose ruins still remain immediately north of the present mill ruins. The Cistercians are renowned for their associations with milling and most monastic settlements of this kind would have had a mill to help make the grange self sufficient. However, no mill is listed among the structures in Monknewtown in the Civil Survey or in the inventories of Mellifont's possessions at the time of the dissolution in 1539. If the Cistercians did operate a mill in Monknewtown, it seems to have disappeared by the mid-sixteenth century. Cartographic sources such as Taylor and Skinner's 1778 map of the area and the estate map of 1766 prepared by Bernard Scalé for Charles Caldwell show no mill on the Mattock in the vicinity of Rossin when both clearly show other mills in the wider area.

Based on the evidence gathered so far, therefore, it seems that Rossin's emergence has nothing to do with mills, certainly not the one that remains upstanding today. So if the name does not owe itself to a mill, to what or whom does it owe its origin? As a placename, Rossin is not unique; there are other Rossins or places with similar names in Ireland including a Rossan near Kinnegad in Co. Meath which was owned by Dudley Loftus and leased to the Gill family during the eighteenth century. The placename 'Rossan' comes from Rosán which indicates a copse or 'small wood'. The large number of trees in Monknewtown in the mid-seventeenth and the mid-eighteenth century were recorded by the Civil Survey and by Arthur Young respectively. It is quite feasible then that at the time the Rossin community emerged, 'the small wood' was an appropriate name for the place.

The time of which we speak, however, still alludes us and we must now turn to addressing one of the most important questions – how and when did Rossin emerge? Scalé's map of 1766 shows a number of structures and groups of structures in the bend of the Boyne but none along the Slane–Drogheda road in what we would call Rossin. It is possible, therefore, that as an actual settlement, Rossin had not begun to develop by 1766 though we know from the lease memorial of 40 years earlier that as a recognized place it was already in existence. Luke Hall's holding in 'Rossen' that contained 'part of Monknewtown' adjacent the main road was bound on the south and west by a much larger holding of over 143 acres which was occupied by Robert and Richard Berrill whose descendants would come to own the public house by 1900. A small plot of land occupied the site that would later become the location of this establishment but for now, it seems to have been an undeveloped one. Also on the eastern side of the Balfaddock Road was a rectangular plot of around 42 acres occupied by Richard Smith at the southern extremity of which was a group of around seven small buildings, probably dwellings. As there are no buildings marked in the area now regarded as Rossin, it would appear that the settlement had not begun to develop or if it had, the dwellings were of insufficient importance or quality to be marked on Scalé's map.

Table 1 is an extract from a rentals list prepared for Charles Caldwell who was himself leasing the lands from the earl of Drogheda.[8] The rentals list, which is dated August 1766 and corresponds to Scalé's map of the same year, appears to relate to holdings in Rossin itself.

Table 1. Rental of lands in the Rossin area, August 1766

Date of lease	*Name*	*Townland*	*Rent* £.	s.	d.
18 Nov 1723	Henry Smith	Balfaddock	20	0	0
17 Nov 17–	Anthony Walsh	Balfaddock	6	3	0
1 April 1740	Henry Smith	Balfaddock	1	2	6
11 July 1745	Robert Berrell & John Evans	Balfaddock	56	15	0
7 Oct 1755	Luke Hall	Balfaddock	14	0	0
30 May 1764	Richard Smith	Balfaddock	30	0	0
11 May 1757	Robert Berrell	Dowth	53	19	0
30 May 1764	John Harpen	Monknewtown	5	0	0

The names listed in Table 1 are probably some of Rossin's earliest tenants who had taken out leases on land along the road from Charles Caldwell but had not begun to develop them in the sense of erecting actual buildings of sufficient size or importance for them to be included on Scalé's map. The oldest buildings in Rossin today, which include Mitchells' pub and some derelict farm buildings, appear to be of eighteenth-century date or to at least incorporate eighteenth-century elements. The tenants listed above are quite possibly the people who first began to build the buildings along the road in Rossin. Their parents, people like Edward Hall who took out the lease in 1724, may have been the founding fathers of Rossin itself. However, being described as 'of Rossen' suggests that the place had originated even before his time, perhaps even during the time of Charles Campbell and the battle of the Boyne, and that at least some people were living there before the turn of the eighteenth century.

Whatever its origins, the community of Rossin was firmly established by the late eighteenth century as demonstrated by those parents who registered their address as Rossin while they were baptising their children rather than the townlands in which they lived officially. However, then as now, it appears to have been recognized as a community only by those who were a part of it. Monknewtown, by the late eighteenth century, was the last remaining Irish estate of the Leinster-born John Baker Holroyd, the earl of Sheffield (1736–1821). The Monknewtown landscape as we know it today developed to a large extent during this century under his tutelage as the relative stability which followed the victory of William III only a few miles downstream provided the necessary climate for long-term improvements and organised estate management. The familiar character of the landscape with its enclosed fields, farms of various sizes, labourers' cottages and wealthy demesnes, became established during this period.[9]

Arthur Young visited Monknewtown in June 1776 and noted details about the soil quality, the hedges, the roads and bridges; the agricultural practices of the tenants; the rental system, and even the living conditions of the poorer labourers. The disadvantages of subletting and over-cultivating the land were particularly described since the tenants of Monknewtown were guilty of both. Young also went into some detail regarding the management and improvements made to the estate by the earl (who lived in England) through his agents on the ground. Sheffield himself visited Ireland in 1762 and found Monknewtown 'as ill used as it possibly could be'. In response, he initiated a programme of improvements which included the signing of several new leases. Young describes some of the earl's initiatives:

> He declined the proposals of several considerable men to take the whole to under-let at rack rents as before, knowing that the same wretched husbandry and poverty must continue if he did, although it would secure his rents most effectually. He … voluntarily engaged to pay for the masonry and principal timber of farm houses, barns, stables, etc. … He made large ditches, planting them with quick round each farm.… He provided an excellent limestone quarry in the neighbourhood, besides lime-kilns on different farms.[10]

These measures contributed to Sheffield's reputation as a great improving absentee landlord.[11] The Monknewtown described above is poor as well as economically and agriculturally backward, though it should be noted that Young's description may be partly biased and slightly exaggerated in order to bolster Sheffield's reputation. Exaggerated or not, Young's theme is reliable in so far as Monknewtown, and presumably Rossin itself, was undergoing a period of development in the mid-eighteenth century. Poverty, seen to be caused by inefficiency and disorganisation, could be overcome by diligence, proper estate management, and general improvements. However, the improvements to the estate were not implemented as smoothly as Sheffield had hoped as the local small farmers were slow to take up leases and were even slower to pay their rents. They were also reluctant to implement Sheffield's reforms, in particular to their dwellings:

> The common farmers, however, prefer living on the ground, surrounded by mud walls, [and] have no idea of the cheerfulness of large windows, but let in barely enough light to do their business through apertures not much better than loop holes; neither has the encouragement to lime been taken advantage of in the degree it might be expected.[12]

It seems that there were serious problems with estate management in Monknewtown during the 1770s, in particular concerning the non-payment of rents and the difficulties in finding suitable tenants. Although the details of the disputes are not actually given, the Sheffield Papers frequently refer to ongoing friction between the tenants and Holroyd's agent, Mr James Boyle. It is worth looking at this period of wrangling in some detail as it shows the endeavours of Sheffield to get his estate in order and reveals much about the relationship between the managers of the estate and the ordinary people on the ground, some of whom, we can be sure, were Rossin residents.

Much of the contents of the Sheffield Papers comprise correspondence between Holroyd and various members of the Foster family of Collon, Co. Louth, a few miles north of Rossin. Dr Thomas Foster, an uncle of John Foster, the last Speaker of the Irish house of commons, recommended James Boyle for the position of agent for Monknewtown. He eventually came to regret this when the estate began to experience difficulties in attracting reliable tenants to take up the new leases. In November 1774, Dr Foster wrote to Sheffield defending Boyle, not knowing 'his equal in the country' and placed the blame for the difficulties at the earl's doorstep:

> Pray, don't lament the state of Monknewtown for I really believe Boyle is doing his best, and I don't see any reason for enlarging his reward for doing his duty. I leave him to tell you what he has done with regard to expense and profit. But how can he let the lands if you have fixt a price which substantial tenants will not give? My brother, W.F., and he is a wise man of the world [allowed] from last May four shillings an acre in a farm of one hundred and eighty for the sake of a good tenant ... Suppose you let an hundred acres of the worst of the land, continue under his care for three years, and from what I could collect from him, he would make an ample return to you from then; show your tenants what might be done with good management and leave the land at the end of three years in a ten times better condition than he found it. In the mean time ... let off the remainder as well as you can and make sure of wealthy and industrious tenants who will stick to the soil.[13]

Sheffield ignored this advice and did nothing to lower the rents and Dr Foster's son, John Thomas Foster, was compelled to make the same points to the earl the following month. John reported that 'it is generally thought that your lands are held up at too high a value'.[14] The previous April, the Speaker himself, had excitedly reported to Sheffield the passing of his latest Corn Laws in the Irish house of commons which had granted a bounty on the overland transport and export of corn with new restrictions being place on imports. He proudly declared that, as a result, 'Monknewtown and all our lands near Drogheda will keep up their rents now beyond a doubt'.[15]

Sheffield, therefore, was getting conflicting information from his cousins back in Ireland. On the one hand, he was being told that tenants could not afford to pay the rents on the recently reorganised and much improved Monknewtown estate because the rents were beyond their means while on the other hand he was being told by one of the most politically important men in the country that there should be no problems in maintaining rents once the new bounty on corn had come into effect because the farmers themselves would be better off. Sheffield chose to listen to Speaker Foster instead of his other relatives and decided not to lower the rents on his estate. The Speaker's comments regarding the collection of rents proved over-optimistic, however, and Sheffield's estate continued to be beleaguered with problems.

In April 1775, John Thomas Foster briefly brought the subject up again and admitted that the agent Boyle, his father's choice, 'has not put forth all his powers' to address the issue.[16] That November, Dr Foster consulted Boyle who assured him that it was through no fault of his own that they were experiencing problems finding tenants to take up leases on the estate and that even the tenants they had were refusing to co-operate. Boyle insisted that:

> … he wished to let all the lands etc. as soon as possible, and that it was not his fault that he did not succeed; that there were two tenants who take what pains they can to be troublesome, I forget their names but he has given you an account of them.[17]

Having lost all faith in Boyle, Sheffield became anxious that a new agent be found to remedy the dilemma and manage his estate effectively. Dr Foster, at Sheffield's request, approached another land agent, a man by the name of Dowdall, who expressed an interest in the position but when asked what terms he desired, refused to discuss the matter further until he was more acquainted with the situation. Dr Foster then took it upon himself to humbly offer his own services to the earl and assured him that when the dispute was resolved and reliable tenants were found, there would be no problem collecting the rents. Dr Foster remarked that certain tenants currently in Monknewtown were 'disposed to keep it on foot to have something to complain of, no matter how groundless'.[18]

The dispute had continued for at least two years and would resurface again twenty years later. In January 1790, 13 years after the death of James Boyle, Sheffield was still being urged to install a good agent in the house which he had recently built in Monknewtown.[19] A man called Nicholls who had been managing things and had recently come to blows with four of the tenants, was unable to reside in the area permanently due to other commitments. In March 1794, Speaker John Foster reiterated the urgent need for a new agent to run the Monknewtown estate.[20] Nevertheless, the agricultural production of the estate seems to have remained strong throughout and in the early 1790s

Foster reported to the earl that Monknewtown was plentiful in crops of flax, corn, and potatoes.

Sheffield's problems in Ireland during the 1770s and 1780s were based, in part at least, on the fact that he was an absentee landlord who, despite his apparent good intentions, was unable to administer an efficient estate because of the fact that he was relying on third parties of varying abilities to do this for him. The culpability of the agent, Mr Boyle, is difficult to judge but from most accounts it appears that he did the best he could given that his hands were effectively tied by the instructions of his boss in England, in particular regarding the rents being demanded of the tenants. Although sometimes a little over optimistic, the counsel which the Fosters offered the absentee earl was based firmly on hard-won experience in the running of their own estate which was centred around nearby Collon, a few miles north of Rossin.

Like the majority of the landowners in the area, Foster's acquisitions had come from the Moore family, by then earls of Drogheda, and previous to the Moores, as we have seen, the Cistercian abbey at Mellifont. In the early eighteenth century, the debts which the Moore family had acquired forced them into subletting much of their holdings which is how Caldwell came to be involved in Balfaddock and other townlands in the Rossin area by 1766.[21] The speed with which the Fosters built up their Collon estate has been described as 'a remarkable achievement'. Fairtclough writes than when Anthony Foster took control of the estate in 1750, it was little more than a wilderness with a few tenants struggling for existence. Arthur Young commented following his visit to Collon that before the improvements had begun, 'the cabins and people [were] as miserable as can be conceived'. There were no roads in the entire parish suitable for a carriage and the state of agriculture was lamentable. This description of Collon is remarkably similar to the Monknewtown described by Arthur Young before Sheffield initiated his programme of improvements there. Like Sheffield, the Fosters needed to attract industrious tenants to make the Collon estate as effective as it possibly could be. Rather than altruism, however, the primary motivation for the improvements in Monknewtown were investment-related. Similarly, the Fosters were politicians who represented Louth in parliament and, therefore, relied on the votes which freeholders would bring them.[22]

And so, like Sheffield after him, Foster set out on a programme of road building, drainage, field clearance, and reclamation. In order to improve the fertility of the soil, he established limestone quarries employing up to 80 men working 27 kilns. The newly-improved fields were divided into plots of 10 acres each and distributed amongst reliable, hard-working tenants. He lent them money and livestock to get them started and built 30 new farm houses using lime and stone. By 1776, Collon was abundant in crops of wheat, barley, and oats. Indeed, the Collon estate had become so effective and had created so much employment, that it was actually causing migration from surrounding estates. By the early nineteenth century, Collon was a thriving agricultural machine and Chief Baron Anthony Foster had won himself the reputation of being 'the great improver' just like Sheffield for the revolution which he oversaw, albeit from a distance, in Monknewtown.[23]

The Collon estate was an agricultural, and on a small parochial scale, an industrial, success story which entitled the Fosters to dispense advice to Sheffield regarding the Monknewtown estate. In the words of Arthur Young, the Fosters had made a 'barren wilderness smile with cultivation, planted it with people and made those people happy.' Most importantly, the Fosters were hands-on landlords who carefully chose their tenants and personally managed their own estate affairs. The earl of Sheffield, as we have seen, was an absentee landlord and although he too brought great improvements to Monknewtown, probably in direct consultation with the Fosters, his personal absence prevented the kind of efficient estate which the Fosters seemed to have achieved. Nevertheless, the Fosters had undoubtedly helped the earl to largely put his Irish affairs in order and to transform the Monknewtown landscape forever.

Based on other documentary and cartographic evidence, it has been shown that Rossin as a settlement appears to have emerged in the second half of the eighteenth century during the time that these improvements were underway. What distinguishes Rossin from other settlements in the area, however, is that by the early nineteenth century at least, it was not just a farming community. Other activities took place here, one of which was the sale and consumption of alcohol. There is little doubt that one of the key elements of the Rossin community today is the public house, known officially as 'The tourist's rest' (a reference to the large amount of trade formerly brought into the area by visitors to the passage tombs) but known to locals as 'Mitchells' after Dolly and Lev Mitchell, recent owners. Architecturally, the building itself appears to have started life sometime in the eighteenth century as one or more single-storey thatched cottages (fig. 5).

A letter in the Sheffield Papers records that in 1807, two decades before the building of Rossin Mill, a Mr Carolan of Monknewtown applied for a licence. Exactly what kind of licence is not mentioned but inference from the rest of the letter suggests that it was a licence to sell alcohol. Another Monknewtown tenant had held a similar licence recently which he took with him when he moved to another part of the neighbourhood. Mr Carolan was keen to fill the vacancy left behind by this individual's departure and appears to have taken his case to his ultimate landlord, the earl of Sheffield. Sheffield, however, was not the person to make the decision though he did put in a good word for him to those whose decision it was:

> I have [had] negotiations for some time with Mr Balfour on this subject through my sister, but without the least success, and I cannot [see why] there should be the least difficulty. I think you might settle it in a

5 Mitchells' pub (July 2000).

> moment by a line to Lord Conyngham as his friend, for I understand the magistrates at Slane decide this business and that there is some tardying here. I am told that Carolan is a very proper person to be licensed.[24]

If this does relate to a licence to sell alcohol, we cannot be not certain that Carolan operated from the same premises we encounter in Griffith's Valuation in the 1850s and which continues to serve the people of Rossin to this day. The doubt arises in part from the fact that the modern establishment is on the south side of the road in Balfaddock while Carolan was from Monknewtown which is located on the north side of the road. There is, however, more than a good chance that it is the same establishment. First, it is Carolan who is described as being from Monknewtown, not the premises. More importantly, as we have already seen on Bernard Scalé's map of 1766, the boundary between Monknewtown and Balfaddock has changed slightly since the eighteenth century. On Scalé's map, parts of Monknewtown do occur on the south side of the Slane–Drogheda road and these small portions may have been cut off from the rest of Monknewtown when the road was constructed, probably sometime during the eighteenth century as it does not seem to have been in existence in 1690. Townland boundaries did not become fixed until the Ordnance Survey of Ireland came into being in the 1830s and it is possible that the site of the public house in 1807 was officially in the Monknewtown part of Rossin rather than in Balfaddock. It is entirely plausible, therefore, that Mitchell's pub has been serving Rossin locals since the late eighteenth century at the earliest and that in the early nineteenth century the landlord was a man by the name of Carolan. Regardless of where the establishment was precisely, this is evidence of activity outside farming and is characteristic of a nucleated, almost village-like settlement, rather than a dispersed rural community. It also indicates that there was more for people in Rossin to do than there was in the wider townlands during the late eighteenth and early nineteenth centuries, one expression of the shifting human focus from its traditional location at Dowth Manor.

As well as social needs, educational and spiritual requirements could also be satisfied in Rossin before the end of the eighteenth century. The existing Catholic chapel in Rossin was built in the mid-nineteenth century on the site of an earlier chapel which was a single-storey slated building located 22 perches (a little over a hundred metres) northwest of the mill site (fig. 6). This chapel must have served not only the parish of Monknewtown but also Dowth which had been without an official church of its own since the 1641 Rebellion. It was during a service in Rossin chapel in late 1799 that the people of the area were first informed of the imminent union with Britain. John Foster, who was totally against the Union, wrote to the earl of Sheffield in December of that year, telling him that the priest in 'Monknewtown' attempted to put the lord lieutenant's proposals to the congregation. 'They professed ignorance. He could not explain and they went away,' Foster recounted.[25] One wonders if their 'ignorance' was feigned to cloak their true feelings on the matter! Be that as it may, this episode demonstrates that the people of Rossin not only had a chapel before the end of the eighteenth century, but that they were being informed of and were expressing opinions in nationally-important political affairs as well.

Tombstone evidence shows that, in addition to a chapel, Monknewtown also had some form of school in the eighteenth century. James Nugent, who died in 1794, was described on his headstone as 'schoolmaster of the parish'. It appears then that the spiritual and educational facilities available to the residents of Rossin in the mid-nineteenth century both had their eighteenth-century predecessors.

The most expensive, most significant and most conspicuous development in the entire history of Rossin was the building of Rossin Mill and it is the immediate background to this event that we turn to consider now. There had been mills in bend of the Boyne since the time of Cormac Mac Airt and especially when the Cistercians of nearby Mellifont farmed the land. The mills of the Boyne valley, as with mills anywhere else, have always been important to their surrounding communities as a destination for their agricultural produce

6 Rossin chapel and former National School (July 2000).

and as a source of flour. The building of Rossin Mill in the 1820s was, therefore, a culmination of a tradition of milling on the River Mattock that extended back into medieval times. Rossin Mill's place in a longer tradition of milling also parallels Rossin's place in a longer tradition of settlement.

The Civil Survey for both Monknewtown and Dowth noted that in the mid-seventeenth century it was the latter parish which possessed mills. When the Ordnance Survey were mapping the area in 1836, they recorded the presence of two corn mills on the Mattock in Dowth parish; one in the townland of the same name and the other in Proudfootstown. Both mills had overshot wheels which powered two pairs of stones.[26] Although these mills were important to the surrounding communities, they were to be dwarfed by the huge complex which would be erected in Monknewtown where the River Mattock meets the main road between Slane and the port town of Drogheda.

There were many factors which contributed to the desire to establish a large-scale milling enterprise in Rossin. One of these was the development of the Boyne Navigation from the mid-eighteenth century onwards which gave a tremendous boost to the production of flour in the area. Barges from Drogheda transported timber, slate and coal to Slane and beyond and returned with corn from the fields and flour from the mills back to the port of Drogheda.[27] In the 1760s a 'very extensive' flour mill was built in Slane with seven pairs of stones capable of grinding 1,000 barrels of corn per week.[28] It had been built by an English miller called David Jebb and Arthur Young had seen nothing like it in England:

> The raising of the mill and offices complete cost £20,000, and has established, in a fine corn country, a constant market; and has preserved the tillage of the neighbourhood, which would have declined on the premium for distant carriage.[29]

Young's insight here is interesting. When Speaker Foster successfully introduced the bounty on corn in the 1770s, he assured the earl of Sheffield that he would have no more problems in collecting rents from his tenants in Monknewtown because of the boost the legislation would provide for corn growers in the Drogheda area. As we have seen, however, the Corn Laws were not the solution Sheffield was looking for and his estate difficulties continued. Young reveals in the above extract that tillage in the neighbourhood of Slane actually suffered because of the bounty, at least at first. The market became saturated with grain and there were too few mills in Ireland initially to process it all. The arrival of Jebb's mill in Slane, therefore, provided a local market for the farmers of the area and 'preserved the tillage of the neighbourhood'.

John Baker Holroyd, earl of Sheffield, was a man who wrote extensively on Irish agriculture and economics and he would have watched the early success of Slane Mill with great interest. However, he was opposed to the first attempts to build a similar establishment on his Irish estate, publicly at least. One of the earliest references to the proposed building of Rossin Mill is in a letter which the earl wrote to Speaker John Foster's son, Col. Thomas Foster, in September 1809. Sheffield had been approached by William Rodgers, a Drogheda miller, who proposed to build a large mill in Monknewtown similar to the one in Slane. Sheffield seemed furious:

> I have always heard that the Irish nation are particularly endowed with assurance, sometimes vulgarly called impudence. Mr Rodgers' measure seemed to me to partake of that quality … I am directed that [the mill] should be obstructed by all means possible. A millrace cannot be formed without raising a weir … Much damage will ensue to the neighbouring land, especially where the unruly river Mattock is in greatness … I have always had a contemplation to build a mill on that part of the river where on both sides [the land] belongs to me. I do not recommend where it is that Mr. Rodgers proposes to build a mill but when I return to Sheffield Place I will send a sketch of the river, part of my survey, on which the position may be marked and returned to me, and it should also be represented whether the banks on both sides be high or low. When these points are ascertained, I can reply better.[30]

Although he cited technical objections, the earl seemed more irritated by the fact that someone else stood to profit from a mill on the Mattock in Monknewtown and it appears that although he actually supported the idea, he would only allow it to proceed on his terms. One question which the letter raises is who was directing the earl to obstruct the venture? Was it English interests who could not stomach the thought of another substantial Irish mill to equal the enormous enterprise in the nearby village of Slane which was already bigger than anything previously built in either country? Perhaps Sheffield was taking advice from his cousins in Collon once more, the Fosters. Having already proven themselves experts in estate management and promoting local industry, the Fosters were also armchair millwrights. In a letter written to William Marshall, Esq., on 2 October 1819, John Foster expressed his concern regarding the millwright's work on Foster's new mill in Collon and drew particular attention to his 'fears that the rollers are too weighty and the flutes of them much too distant and course'.[31]

As it turned out, 1809 was actually a good time to build a flour mill in Meath as the account books of Jebb's Mill in Slane indicate (fig. 7).[32] Milling in the early nineteenth century was certainly a very healthy business for Jebb's Mill at Slane. By 1823, his mill was supplying flour to bakers as far away as Ardee, Armagh, Strokestown, Kingscourt, Edgeworthstown, Clones, Dublin and Enniskillen, as well as to those in towns closer to home such as Drogheda, Collon, Navan and Slane itself.[33] In the previous decade, the mill was also making payments to ships bound for Liverpool which suggests that wheat from the Slane area, including that grown in the fields around Rossin, was supplying bakers in England with their flour as well.

Whatever the reason for Sheffield's reluctance in 1809 – the potential of being beaten to it, the pressures of his peers in England, well-intended but overly-cautious financial advice from the Fosters, or legitimate concerns about the negative impacts of a poorly thought-out venture on the land which directed his conscience to oppose the project – the earl refused Rodgers permission to build a mill at this time.

As we have already seen, the mill eventually began life in 1825 with the lease agreement between the next earl of Sheffield, George Holroyd, and Townley Blackwood Hardman of Drogheda. Having acquired the site for a mill pond on land previously held by Widow Fernan and a three-acre site for the mill complex itself on land formerly held by Patrick Drew, Hardman signed a lease with Sheffield for three named lives renewable forever on 22 October 1825. The lease refers to one of the Corn Laws, an act of parliament passed in the 25th year of the reign of King George III (1784–5) which was designed to encourage the building of corn mills without adversely affecting agricultural production. This act allowed leases to be drawn up between the owner and the tenant for the erection of a mill and associated developments such as mill ponds and millraces, provided that the sites in question were not part of the landowner's private demesne and that the areas in question did not amount to more than three acres.

A 'good bridge' had to be built within one year and the mill itself within two years of the signing of the lease, (i.e. before October 1827) at Hardman's

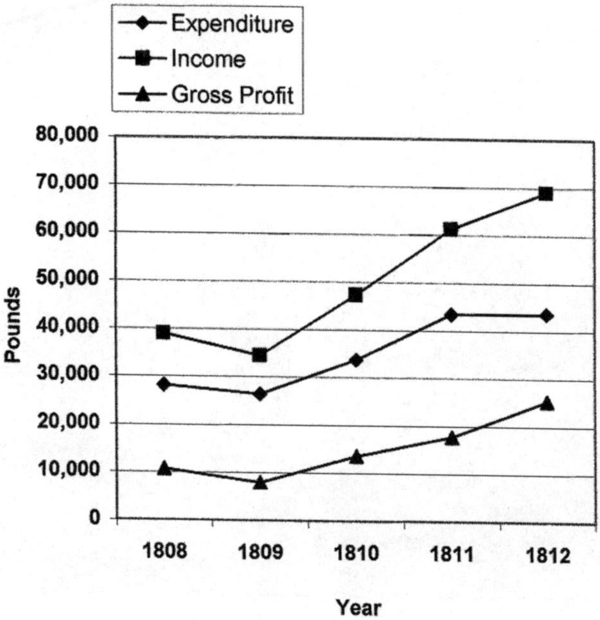

7 Slane mill accounts, 1808–12.

own expense, and at least £10 per acre was to be spent on the grounds. The lease recommended that he spend £1,200 on the development in total. The highest rent was to be charged for this land (£5 per acre annually) and half of the annual rent was to be paid as a fine upon each renewal of the lease. As part of the enterprise, Hardman would be allowed to make use of the Mattock river and the nearby stream and workers would be permitted to cross Sheffield's land in order to get to work. According to Lyons, a total of £7,000 was eventually spent building Rossin Mill and its associated premises. With a 30-horsepower waterwheel system, it was good for at least eight months of the year and by 1837, steam power was introduced to act as a backup during periods when the river was low. A 'neat five storey building in good repair', it had six pairs of stones (three for oats and three for wheat) and storage space for between four and six thousand barrels.[34] It also boasted three kilns for drying the corn before grinding.[35]

It should not surprise us that a substantial mill was erected here, particularly when one considers the topography and infrastructure of the immediate area. Many commentators have testified to the excellent quality of farmland here. In August 1793, Foster reported to Sheffield 'never was there a more promising appearance in corn, flax and potatoes' as there was in Monknewtown at that time.[36] Thompson's *Statistical survey of Co. Meath* was

8 Rossin Mill in the 1850s.

written at the behest of the earl of Sheffield himself and published in 1802. He noted that the area around Drogheda was particularly suitable for large quantities of red wheat, rye, oats and barley.[37] The Ordnance Survey described Monknewtown's road network in detail and praised it for facilitating agriculture and communication. Monknewtown, therefore, had the natural resources, the necessary manpower, and access to a developing transport network, which would all ensure a successful enterprise, at least in its early decades.

The mill did not create the community of Rossin as was previously believed, however. Although neither Foster nor Sheffield make any reference to Rossin, the mill was built in an area which had been known to the locals as Rossin for at least a century. Nor would the mill have provided direct employment to any large degree, though it would have benefited the locals by providing a direct destination for their agricultural produce and by providing farm labourers around Rossin with a livelihood in tillage so long as the mills required grain. The great flour mills in Slane and Rossin were not textile mills that relied on a large workforce. These buildings were more like giant warehouses than bustling factories. Technological advances in the milling industry during the second half of the eighteenth century included improved cast-iron shafting and waterwheels and more advanced gearing systems which allowed a single waterwheel to power more than one set of stones. The wheel could also power other mechanisms such as fans for drying the grain and elevators for transporting it from one level of the complex to the next. Such automation allowed even the largest mills to operate with a minimum number of employees. Although the larger enterprise in Slane had kept farmers in over a ten mile radius around Slane busy since the 1760s, it only directly employed a dozen or so people. In one week in April 1827, the year in which Rossin Mill was due to open, Jebb's mill in Slane paid a total of £225 0*s*. 10*d*. for wheat but in that same week, it spent a paltry £1 8*s*. 8*d*. on labour.[38] At the turn of the nineteenth century, a miller from Navan boasted that he could raise a barrel of wheat every two minutes without the cost of a single labourer to carry it.[39]

Although the arrival of the mill in Rossin did not directly create many jobs, it must have had an enormous psychological impact on the local community, similar to that a modern community would experience today with the arrival of an industrial estate in their back garden. It must also have been an exciting time for Rossin in many ways. Here was an enormous new flour factory being built in a small relatively new community; a building of the kind which would only have been previously seen by them in the town of Drogheda or in the village of Slane. Unfortunately, there are no publicly-available sources describing the psychological impact of the mill's establishment on the community but one direct effect of which we are aware, however, is the loss of the holy well in Monknewtown. The well had been located close to the mill site and was venerated at each pattern day until the mill's arrival.[40] Why the practice ceased after the mill's construction is difficult to say. Perhaps it was an expression of the locals' disapproval of such an overpowering edifice being erected on their doorsteps. Perhaps the land immediately around the mill was private property and locals felt intimidated going to the well, scared away by the 'wicked caretaker' who lived in the mill yard. Whatever the reason, the arrival of the great mill in Rossin was both a new beginning and the end of an era for its inhabitants.

3. Growth and decline: Rossin in the nineteenth century

Records relating to the day-to-day running of Rossin Mill itself do not appear to be publicly available at present, so in order to obtain some insight into the operation of the business, we must turn instead to the nearby Slane Mill which was of similar size though established much earlier. Between 1824 and 1828, the period in which Rossin Mill was built, labourers at Slane were paid between 10*d.* and 2*s.* per day.[1] In 1808, a typical year for Slane Mill before the Great Famine, the account books record substantial amounts of money being spent on 832 sacks and 2,276 bags amounting to £442 19*s.* 9*d.* Money to the amount of £343 8*s.* 11*d.* was paid to the Boyne Navigation for transport to and from the nearby port town of Drogheda and other purchases included flour casks, horses, carts, and cars. A total of 135 tons of coal in that year cost the business £229 11*s.* 7*d.* and charges by Drogheda's warehouses came to £174 5*s.* 5½*d.* By far the most substantial expense, of course, was the wheat, barley and oats brought in from farms over a ten mile radius of Slane which in 1808 came to £26,259 8*s.* 5*d.* The total outgoings of Slane Mill in that year were £28,243 13*s.* 6*d.* but business was booming with sales amounting to £38,938 13*s.*, leaving a gross profit of around £10,695 to be divided between its directors, David Jebb, Marquis Conyngham and Townley Balfour.[2]

By 1836, the relatively new mill in Rossin had passed into the hands of William Rodgers of Drogheda, the same miller who had proposed to build a mill in Monknewtown as far back as 1809 when Slane Mill was enjoying steady growth. As we have seen, Monknewtown's landlord at that time, John Baker Holroyd, regarded Rodgers' proposals as 'impudent'. Sixteen years later, John's son George, the next earl, was approached by another Irish gentleman, Townley Blackwood Hardman who was more successful in his aims. And now, Rodgers found himself tenant miller in the enterprise which he himself initially envisaged. During the mill's early years, Rossin would have enjoyed good business since in the mid-1830s, 80 per cent of British grain imports came from Ireland.[3] This ensured that agricultural activity in Ireland remained geared towards tillage rather than pasture. If Slane Mill had to draw corn from up to ten miles away, then Rossin Mill, being of similar size, must surely have had a similar catchment area.[4]

The large milling enterprises in Rossin and Slane did not absolutely dominate the milling industry in the locality, however. There was still business enough, before the Great Famine (1845–50) at least, to support the smaller traditional mills in the area. Dowth parish, which had corn mills long before the coming of Rossin Mill in the 1820s, still had two operational mills in 1836: Elcock's Mill in Dowth and Drew's Mill in Proudfootstown. Both were much smaller affairs than Rossin of course, being one-storey thatched buildings in good repair with a single overshot wheel powering two pairs of stones. Like Rossin Mill, they both drew their power from the Mattock.[5] In local terms, the main difference between Rossin Mill and the smaller mills in Dowth was their markets. While the small mills would have met the demand for flour locally, Rossin Mill would have sent much of its produce further afield. The large mills, like those of Slane and Rossin, were international concerns even during their construction as they were usually built by Englishmen. David Jebb, who built and ran Slane Mill, was brought over especially from England by Marquis Conyngham of Slane and Townley Balfour of Oldbridge. As a large mill, it purchased grain from local farmers, dried it in kilns and then sold the flour to bakers all around Ireland as well as on overseas markets. Rossin Mill would have operated in much the same way.

Although Dowth maintained its smaller milling establishments and although its farmers profited from the agricultural demands of two great and two small mills, the main focus of human activity in the area had, by the mid-nineteenth century, almost entirely shifted to Rossin. By 1836, Rossin comprised a concentrated linear settlement boasting a public house, a chapel, a school, and one of the largest flour mills in the county. By the 1880s at least, Rossin also had a dispensary which was funded by the poor rate to provide basic medical care, including vaccinations, to the residents of Rossin and to the wider community.[6] When taken collectively, these services and facilities arguably earn Rossin the title of 'village' so often given it by the grand jury during the first half of the nineteenth century. In fact, the grand jury even referred to Rossin as a town on occasion, though the term would have had been used much more liberally in the first half of the nineteenth century than we would use it today.

Nevertheless, what seems to have been little more than a number of empty plots of land in the mid-eighteenth century held under lease from Campbell and later Caldwell of Newgrange and Holroyd, earl of Sheffield, in England, had in the space of a century become a modest rural settlement with many of the facilities associated with village life. But Rossin, then as now, continued to be known almost exclusively to those who lived there. Although all the structures were shown of course, the settlement was generally not labelled as Rossin on Ordnance Survey maps of the area. An exception, however, was a rare appearance on the one-inch map of 1899–1902 which was produced for the growing tourism industry in Ireland at that time (fig. 1).

As we have already seen, there are very few direct references to Rossin written by outsiders which implies that Rossin was a community recognised only by those who were actually a part of it. One of the reasons for this was probably the fact that the settlement itself was small and still quite a new one and that Rossin as a notion was then, as now, largely an abstract phenomenon. Apart from parish registers and newspaper advertisements where the information would have been supplied by the residents themselves, the official placenames are almost invariably used by outsiders to describe the area. For example, when the *Drogheda Argus* published the minutes of the Dunleer presentment sessions in May 1861, they related a debate on the plans to rebuild 'Mattock Bridge on the road from Drogheda to Slane by Dowth'.[7] Rossin was well established by the 1860s and the only reason why any geographical description of the Mattock Bridge would omit a reference to Rossin and instead refer to the townland of Dowth, would be the fact that very few people outside the community would ever have heard of Rossin let alone know where it was. The situation is still very much the same today.

Nevertheless, to the people who lived there, Rossin was a very real community with facilities to meet their social, medical, educational and spiritual needs. The chapel and school would have been two of the facilities central to community life in Rossin in the nineteenth century. The Roman Catholic chapel in its present form, known officially as 'Our Lady of the Assumption', was erected during the administration of two parish priests whose terms ran from 1838 to 1862.[8] However, as discussed in the previous chapter, there has been a chapel on this site since at least the end of the eighteenth century, long before the coming of Rossin Mill. Griffith's Valuation of 1854 recorded that the chapel was the property of the earl of Sheffield but what Griffith did not note was that, like the mill, the school, and Mattock Bridge below it, the name 'Rossin' was being applied to this chapel by locals. The parish school and the schoolmaster's dwelling in Monknewtown, located immediately west of the chapel, were also owned by the earl and both buildings were exempt from Poor Law rate payments as they did not produce a profit for their owner. In all, three of the main buildings in Rossin (mill, church and school) were on Sheffield's land on the north side of the Slane–Drogheda road while the public house, dispensary and most of the dwellings in Rossin were along the south side of the road on land leased from Patrick Drew of Monknewtown and Gradwell of Dowth.[9]

Prior to the coming of the national school, Luke Dunne educated the local children in what has been referred to as a 'hedge school' though in reality classes would have been conducted in the school house listed by Griffith.[10] By 1866, a new school building had been erected from parish funds and shortly afterwards, education in Rossin came under state funding and control through the Commissioners of National Education. The national school was conducted in the new school house which was annexed to the chapel. This building, measuring 22 by 14 feet, was slated and had three windows. Built from rubble masonry, it was a one-room building which was adequately ventilated and warmed by a fireplace. The internal door which had connected chapel and school had been 'permanently closed up' prior to the application for grant assistance in an attempt to conform to the national school system requirements to separate religious denomination and education. The application for national school status for Monknewtown was made by the parish priest of Slane, Fr P. Callary, on 19 July 1866. The application form tells us that over a six-month period prior to the application, a total of 20 boys and 30 girls had been attending this school and that this was already the limit for which the building could cater. There were four eight-foot desks and forms, a small blackboard, but no clock.

Monknewtown National School was established in Rossin at the beginning of August 1866 and three weeks later it was visited by the district inspector, Edward Mac Creanor, who commented that 'the house, furniture ... and teacher are sufficient' and that 'this is likely to be a very useful school.' All the children of the neighbourhood were to attend and the school was to be open to children of all religious backgrounds, though at that time the entire population of Monknewtown was Roman Catholic. When he had met some of the heads of households in the area, the inspector had been informed that they were 'all anxious to have a female National School in Monknewtown.' The pupils had to pay 1*d*. or 2*d*. per quarter to attend the school although poor children were admitted free of charge.

On its first day as a National School, the former hedge school master, Luke Dunne, retired and was replaced by Ellen Clarke who had previously been the senior paid monitor of Slane national school's females. She was described by the inspector as a woman of good character with 'fair' methods of conducting school but she had received 'no instruction on the art of teaching' and could produce no testimonies to prove her fitness for office. Among future masters and mistresses would be John Ogle of Rossin, a member of a relatively well-off farming family, and Mary B. Tully whose descendants continue to live in the school house today.[11]

One of the things that strikes us when examining the development of Rossin is the way in which settlement in the area changed depending on the circumstances of the time. As discussed the first chapter, Rossin was in some respects a successor of the grange of Monknewtown which developed over time into a hamlet. The Anglo-Norman borough of Dowth, on the other hand, had declined in importance since the 1640s and by the late eighteenth century, the focus for human activity in the bend of the Boyne was concentrated in other places, most importantly Rossin. But although Rossin had facilities unavailable in other parts of the area, such as a working school, a chapel, a public house and a dispensary, there were still facilities in Dowth which Rossin lacked during the nineteenth century. By the 1880s, for instance, there was a post office in Dowth opposite Dowth Hall but there is never any mention of a post office in Rossin in documentary or cartographic sources (not that this necessarily means that one did not exist) even though it was located on the mailcoach road between Slane and Drogheda. By far the most noticeable structure in Dowth, however, apart from Dowth Hall itself, was the Netterville Institution. In 1826, the sixth Viscount Netterville bequeathed Dowth Castle, his fifteenth-century tower house, and 60 acres of land for the use of widows and orphans together with an annual sum for their maintenance. The bequest, almost certainly prompted by the impact of the Napoleonic Wars, was made in a will drawn up on 29 July 1812 and stated the following in characteristic Victorian style:

> I desire that these stables and offices belonging to the castle next Drogheda be made comfortable and kept so for six poor desolate honest widows and six orphans, who when of proper age, are to be apprenticed with such a moderate sum as my executors shall think proper and others got in their place, and the widows likewise to be replaced when they die or are turned out for bad conduct or improper behaviour.[12]

In 1836, there were four only widows living in the castle but the numbers steadily increased.[13] In 1877, funds from the Netterville trust enabled the widows and orphans to be moved out of the tower house and into a new building, a substantial gothic mansion beside the original castle that continued to accommodate them into the twentieth century. In addition to accommodation, the Netterville Charitable Institution had provided a school for the orphans' education and catered for the other children of Dowth as well. This school was in operation by 1844[14] and its most famous pupil was the celebrated Fenian and poet, John Boyle O'Reilly, whose parents both taught there. The school was leased to the Commissioners of Education but had closed down by 1866 when Monknewtown School in Rossin became the national school for the entire area.

The Netterville Institute is an example of how developments in an area, regardless of conditions in the wider community, were largely dependant on the will of influential individuals or 'brokers' like the sixth Viscount Netterville. In Rossin, the main brokers were the earls of Sheffield who could obstruct or encourage the development of the community; the Fosters of Collon in the late eighteenth century at least who kept a close eye on estate affairs and advised the earl of the course of action he should or should not take; the entrepreneurs and millers who persisted in their attempts to acquire permission to the build the mill; and other men of local importance such as those who helped the grand jury decide whether or not money should be spent on maintaining the local infrastructure such as the roads and bridges.

As a result of the efforts of the grand jurists in particular, the transport of corn and flour to and from Rossin Mill was so much easier. Indeed, the road network in and around Rossin played a vital role in the development of this community. The mail coach road serving Slane, Drogheda, Navan and then on to Enniskillen, bisected Rossin from east to west while the Duleek–Collon road entered Dowth by the castle and left the area through Mellifont. The most important road for the mill would be the road to Drogheda which, along with the Boyne Navigation, allowed flour to be transported to the port and from there to the markets of England. The shift in human activity from other parts of the bend of the Boyne to Rossin between the 1830s and 1860s was also due, in part at least, to the location of Rossin on the main Slane–Drogheda road. Indeed, the road itself may have been one of the main factors in the foundation of the settlement, perhaps during the first half of the eighteenth century. The parish registers for the first half of the nineteenth century and the successive editions of Ordnance Survey maps, indicate that there was a sustained concentration of population here throughout the nineteenth century. Because most people in the locality lived in Rossin and because Rossin was located on the intersection of the main Slane–Drogheda road with roads from Dowth, Balfaddock and the Littlewood of Slane, it was an obvious choice for the upgraded school and chapel as it was convenient for the wider community and not just to those who considered themselves Rossin residents.

The roads were continually maintained by the grand jury who allocated considerable sums for the purpose at every session although the amounts dropped dramatically in the post-Famine period.[15] The overseers whose duty it was to acquire the materials, organise the labourers, and pay their wages, were drawn from the wealthier families of the district, such as the Drews, the Ogles, and the Elcocks, who were well established in Rossin by the early nineteenth century. Other overseers were relatively new arrivals, such as Richard Maguire of Newgrange and William Wynne of Dowth. Lord Netterville and the local clergy also served. In the mid-nineteenth century, Maguire of Newgrange and Gradwell of Dowth Hall, as well as the Drews and the Berrills of Rossin, were among the cess payers of the area. This was an indication of their wealth and social standing and it entitled them to sit on the grand jury during sessions in Navan.

For the majority of people in Rossin and the surrounding district during the nineteenth century, including the upper echelons of local society, the rhythm of life was rooted firmly in agriculture as livelihoods and wealth were based on the land as they had been for thousands of years. During harvest time, readers of Drogheda newspapers would see notices of auctions of farm produce in many parts of Louth and Meath including the Rossin area. For example, in July 1861, Thomas Maguire, Esq., advertised the upcoming auction of crops and hay in Crewbaun a short distance west of Rossin. He offered 15 acres of excellent oats and sixty cocks of prime hay. He also advertised the sale of 30 acres of potato oats at Newgrange which, he claimed, were 'the finest in the country'.[16] Around the same time, there were 11 cocks of hay to be bought in Dowth and towards the end of the following month, a sale of oats and hay at Monknewtown 'adjoining Rossin Mills' was advertised.[17]

At 1 p.m. on 28 November 1861, in Monknewtown close to Rossin Mills on the Slane Road, Mr Malcolm would sell 20 acres of prime land for a crop of oats, fifteen tons of clover hay in pikes, three acres of prime swede turnips, a large quantity of straw, and a gig with cushions etc.[18] The auction of the personal effects of Thomas Elcock, a small farmer from Ballinacrad, Dowth, had taken place in January 1861. The items up for sale give a further insight into agricultural life of the area in post-Famine times. His effects included corn, a 'splendid mare fit for any harness', a two-year old filly sired by 'Young Sir Harry', Mr P. Kirk's horse in Crewbaun; a dray and harness; a few sheep; two pigs; cows and calves; ploughs, harrows, ten tons of the best upland hay; four stacks of prime white oats; and several other articles which Elcock left behind.[19]

Rossin does not seem to have been home to any particularly powerful landowners during the nineteenth century. There were families in and around Rossin who occupied the middle ground socially and these were connected by blood and marriage as demonstrated through a brief examination of the parish registers for the area. The Elcocks, Drews and Ogles, for instance, all of whom took leading roles in the Rossin community as relatively wealthy farmers, millers and overseers, were closely connected through kinship and friendship. Although it is difficult to gain an insight into their feelings towards one another from available sources, the fact that they would often become godfather or godmother to each other's children is some indication of how the close-knit Rossin community operated in the nineteenth century.

Those in the upper levels of society, such as the Maguires of Newgrange and the Gradwells of Dowth, often looked elsewhere for suitable matches when it came to marriage. The most extreme example of this was Robert Gradwell of Dowth Hall who married the daughter of an earl at the turn of the twentieth century.[20] But even the Gradwells played a role in the Rossin community despite their aloof social standing, albeit from a distance. They were heavily involved in local affairs such as the administration of the poor law system which ran the dispensary in Rossin and in public works such as the improvements to the Mattock Bridge in the 1860s. So although men of the calibre of Robert Gradwell, John Foster, and the earl of Sheffield did not live in Rossin, they always had a profound impact on its development and day-to-day affairs. The most influential man in Rossin itself during the nineteenth century was James Drew of Monknewtown who in 1841 was a warden for Mellifont electoral division under the Drogheda poor law union board of guardians.[21] Drew was a relatively-strong farmer and landlord to many of Rossin's residents. As a cess payer, William Rodgers, the primary tenant on the lease for Rossin Mill, was also a man of some stature in the community and this may be a reflection of the mill's early success as a business.

Unfortunately, Rossin Mill suffered a severe case of bad timing and Rodgers' initial success began to slip away in the post-Famine period. When Slane Mill was completed in 1767, it enjoyed the favourable conditions of its time and these were conducive to a successful milling enterprise. First, there was the boost which the milling industry of the area received from the recent development of the Boyne Navigation and a further boost soon came in the form of John Foster's Corn Law which gave bounties on grain and flour destined for the Dublin market. There were the technological advances in the milling industry which arose from the industrial revolution in England that allowed large operations to exist efficiently with a minimum number of employees. In addition, the global events of the late eighteenth and early nineteenth centuries proved advantageous to the Irish milling industry. The American Revolutionary War (1775–83) and the Napoleonic Wars (1792–1815) made the British markets increasingly reliant on Irish suppliers. Between the turn of the nineteenth century and the 1810s, the percentage of Britain's grain imports from Ireland jumped from just over 16 to 57 per cent.[22] Slane Mill, therefore, was in a position to capitalise on these events because it was, quite literally, in the right place at the right time.

Rossin Mill, on the other hand, which was built between 1825 and 1827, had to deal with challenges from the outset, one of which was the Act of Union. Despite the desperate opposition of John Foster and others, this act came into effect in January 1801 and eventually contributed to a decline in trade during the 1820s and 1830s and to the end of economic expansion in Ireland. That is not to say that the mill never saw good times, of course. During the first half of the nineteenth century, exports of flour increased from 25,000 cwt annually to 750,000 cwt and William Rodgers must surely have prospered.[23] But, towards the end, he must have looked back over his milling career with some feelings of bitterness, in particular at the fact that he had been prevented from building Rossin Mill in 1809 when it could have had fifteen or more years of the good times.

As early as the 1830s, after less than a decade in business in Rossin, Rodgers could see the storm clouds brewing. Agricultural prosperity in Ireland as a whole was in decline with many tenants already terminating their leases and emigrating.[24] By far the most significant impact on the milling industry in Ireland, however, resulted from the Great Famine of 1845–50. Due to an overall decline in population of around two million people nationally, there was a reduced demand for food and a reduced labour force in post-Famine Ireland. This would cause wheat yields to drop by 66 per cent between the 1850s and 1870s; oats by 60 per cent and barley by 33 per cent.[25] From this time on, agricultural activity in Ireland began to turn towards pasture which was less labour intensive. The Rossin area underwent this changeover too and herds' houses and fields of pasture began to appear the during the second half of the nineteenth century, replacing the formerly sprawling wheat fields.

Although there were initial fluctuations, the general depopulation of the bend of the Boyne during and after the Great Famine of the 1840s is a theme which can be replicated for almost every townland and parish in Ireland

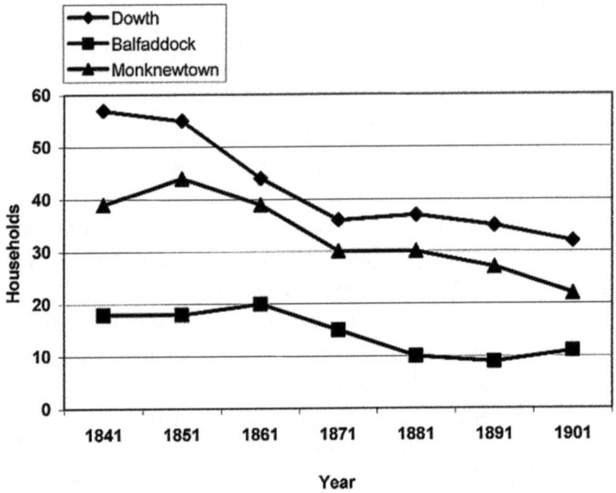

Source: N.A., Census of Ireland 1901

9 Households in the Rossin area, 1841–1901

(figs. 9–10). Before the Famine, Dowth townland had contained nearly 20 more families than Monknewtown which in turn had twenty more than Balfaddock.[26] Of course, townland sizes varied greatly between Balfaddock and the other two but the difference between Monknewtown and Dowth was less than 150 acres. So in the decades before the Famine, at the height of Rossin Mill's production, many more people lived in Dowth townland than in Monknewtown and Balfaddock. However, during the decade 1841–51 when Dowth's population had already begun to decline, half a dozen more families arrived in Monknewtown. This may be an indication of Rossin's continued expansion during the Famine as refugees from the wider rural community sought accommodation along the roadside. During the twenty years between 1851 and 1871, the two townlands experienced a major fall which saw the loss of a third of their families. This depopulation trend was paralleled by a fall off in the production of cereals in Ireland which dropped by between 33 per cent and 60 per cent nationally.

As Rodgers watched the local families pack up and move out, the business began to run aground. Griffith's Valuation of 1854 recorded that Rossin Mill was still by far the most valuable holding in Monknewtown parish, being worth £134. This included the mill itself which was then operated by Richard Hill (a merchant and miller of Drogheda),[27] its associated stores, offices and overseer's house. Two years later, however, in April 1856, the mill was put up

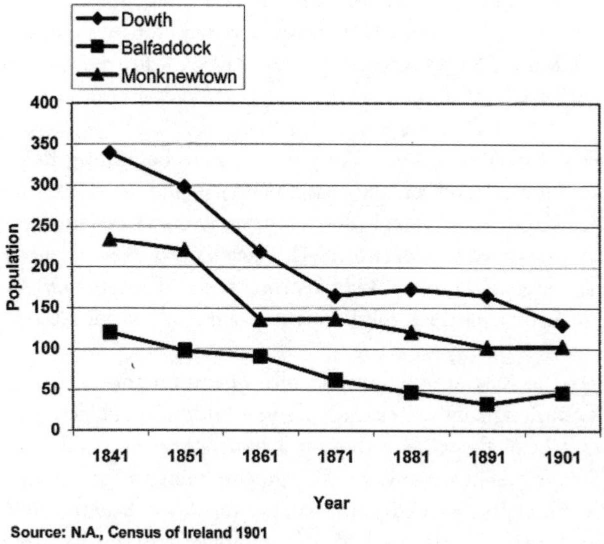

10 Population of the Rossin Area, 1841–1901

for sale by William Rodgers. Unable to get a sufficient price, Rodgers was forced to withdraw the business from the auction. In 1858, Rossin Mill ground to a halt completely and during the following year, it came before the Landed Estates Court, evidence of the debt which Rodgers must have then been in. It was up for sale again on 17 March 1860 but once more, it was withdrawn.

An advertisement had appeared in the *Drogheda Argus* the week before the second auction, giving potential buyers notice of the sale:[28]

> In the matter of the estate of Thomas Binks Wetherall, assignee of William Rodger, owner, exparte the Rev Thomas Fielding Martin, petitioner. … Pursuant to the order of the Landed Estate Court, Mr Robert Bedford Daly, auctioneer, will on Saturday 17th day of March 1860 at the hour of two o'clock afternoon at the Tholsel in the town of Drogheda, sell by public auction in three several lots:–
>
> (1) Premises in Laurence Street and store in Bachelor's Lane in the town of Drogheda held for a term of one life or twenty-one years from 29th September 1858. Profit rent £9.
>
> (2) Lands of Monknewtown with Mills thereon, County of Meath, held under lease of lives renewable forever. Estimate profit rent £236 3*s.* 1*d.*

(3) Lot of ground with buildings thereon situate south side of William Street and at Palace Row, Drogheda, held for thirty-one years from 1 May 1830 with toties quoties covenant for renewal. Profit rent £24 17*s.* 3½*d.*

By now, farmers as well as many millers were beginning to realise that there was no future in cereal crops as a primary land use. Cattle herds were expanding as the most viable alternative to cereal growing though flax production too started to increase. On St Patrick's Day 1860, an advertisement by John P. Kelly of Dunleer Flax Works appeared in the *Drogheda Argus* appealing to farmers in the locality to embrace flax as a viable alternative crop:

> Free trade is now only coming into operation and corn and grain of every kind is likely to be cheap this year but cannot be dearer than it is at present. I can, therefore, with great confidence recommend a large sowing of flax, it being the only product in the kingdom of which there is a deficient supply and opening of the French markets to our yarns and linens at reduced duties will give a great impetus to the demand for flax.[29]

It is illuminating that the above advertisement appeared in the press on the very day that Rossin Mill went up for sale and was hardly an encouragement to prospective buyers. Kelly, of course, had his own very obvious agenda here but he pointed out that the average crop of flax yielded £15–£20 per acre at a time when 'no corn or grain crop will pay much more than half as much'. This was the everyday reality with which cereal farmers and millers were faced: there was simply too much supply in the industry and too little demand. This echoed the problem which Arthur Young referred to a century earlier in the 1760s when there were too few large mills in Ireland to take in the amount of grain which Foster's bounty had generated. This time, however, it was the millers as well as the farmers who were unable to find a market for their produce.

After two years of idleness, Rossin Mill was finally purchased privately in 1861 by none other than the earl of Sheffield himself. This earl was a direct descendant of John Baker Holroyd, the earl who had refused Rodgers permission to build his mill in Rossin in 1809, and descendant also of the next earl, George, who had allowed the mill to be built by Blackwood Hardman and then leased to Rodgers. Having now purchased it himself, the current earl of Sheffield sublet the premises to Wetherhill, Powell and Co. Ltd who were the Drogheda agents for the Royal Insurance Company.[30] The intervention of Wetherhill, Powell & Co. in taking over the faltering mill in 1861 prolonged its life for a few decades more but Rossin Mill never recovered after the Great Famine despite their efforts. Nor did the steady departure of households in the locality cease before the century was out. The same edition of the *Drogheda Argus* that had carried the notice of sale for Rossin Mill in March 1860 also contained numerous advertisements by steam packet companies encouraging people to take the emigrant ships out of Ireland:

> Important to intending emigrants! A return just received from the Canadian Government made by eighty-five municipalities in Canada shows a great demand for labourers and artisans. The following will find immediate employment and good wages: farm labourers, house servants, boys and girls from thirteen to sixteen years of age, blacksmiths, tinsmiths, foundry men, bricklayers, masons, joiners, carpenters, coopers, shoemakers, tailors and miners.[31]

The mill had been closed for two years and local farmers were turning to cattle breeding rather than cereal tillage for which there was no longer a sufficient market. Pastoral agriculture, however, meant that farm labourers would not be required in the numbers that had been necessary in the fields since the second half of the eighteenth century. The depopulation of Monknewtown, Balfaddock and Dowth, therefore, continued and despite the minor variations, the overall population of the Rossin area as a whole was in more or less constant decline throughout second half of the nineteenth century (fig. 10). Balfaddock townland suffered sustained population decline from 1861 onwards though it exhibited some signs of growth in the last decade of the nineteenth century. Dowth alone lost half of its population in just three decades (1841–71) in a dramatic plunge. This fall continued down to the turn of the twentieth century when Monknewtown displayed some small signs of recovery. During the 1870s, things had finally begun to stabilise and Dowth too had even showed some sign of recovery. However, the slow exodus resumed and continued steadily until it eventually met Monknewtown's low level in 1911.

In addition to the national population slump and the reduced demand for cereal produce which this exacerbated, there were other reasons why the great flour mills, including that in Rossin, were no longer profitable, one of which was the repeal of Foster's Corn Law in 1846. It is interesting to note that it was John Foster's Corn Law which had helped to convince his cousin, the earl of Sheffield, that his tenants in Monknewtown would have no difficulty in making their rent payments from then on. The bounty on the land transfer of grain was probably also one of the factors which encouraged John Baker Holroyd to contemplate building a mill in Monknewtown himself in the early years of the nineteenth century. Yet it was the repeal of this law during the Great Famine, by allowing the British markets to import corn from elsewhere, that contributed so significantly to its eventual demise.

Cheaper shipping also contributed to the drop in the price of flour. Another factor in the decline of many of the great mills, including Rossin, was technological. Interestingly again, it was technological advances which had provided a boost to the milling industry during the second half of the eighteenth century and this new technology was employed in Rossin Mill when it was built in the 1820s. By the 1870s, there had been further technological advances such as rollers which were now being used instead of the traditional circular mill stones. Rossin Mill, however, did not convert to the new more speedy and cost-efficient methods and eventually it paid the price for not keeping up with the times.

The Irish milling industry was, therefore, in crisis during the 1870s and 1880s and within a decade two-thirds of the country's flour mills had shut down, victims of a changed national environment.[32] Despite its small size, Proudfootstown Mill in Dowth initially remained valuable in the early post-Famine period. Operated by James Drew on 42 acres of land, it was worth £30 in 1854. When the value of the land is included, the total enterprise was worth £70. This valuation was half that of Rossin Mill which only had nine acres of land attached and relied almost totally on the farmers of the district for grain. Elcock's Mill, also in Dowth townland, was not so fortunate as Drew's and in 1854, it was vacant and valued at a mere pound.[33]

By the turn of the twentieth century, tillage accounted for only a quarter of total agricultural output in Ireland. Grain production would increase occasionally as a response to wartime conditions outside the country (i.e. in 1919, 1933–6 and 1944)[34] but for many of the great flour mills, particularly those like Rossin which failed to keep up with changing technology, their days were numbered after the Great Famine. Wetherhill, Powell and Co. oversaw the Rossin business for 15 years and were the primary tenant in Slane Mill also. In 1877, they were listed in the Valuation Books as just Wetherhill and Powell and, by 1885, only Thomas Wetherhill was left and he persevered until 1899.[35] When the Wetherhill era came to an end at the turn of the twentieth century, Rossin Mill rapidly became a ruin with a valuation of only £10 over the period 1900–21. When the Bretts, a northern textile manufacturing family, took over Rossin Mill in 1935, it followed a period of 13 years since Independence when Rossin Mill had been struck from the valuation book for having no value whatsoever. Like so many other redundant flour mills throughout the country which still had their mechanisms in place, powered by water and steam, Rossin's final chapter saw it used as a flax mill until 1946.[36] Sadly, the end of the Second World War heralded an end to Britain's brief dependency on Irish textile manufacture and Rossin Mill stopped working forever after 120 years of mixed fortunes. It was later stripped of its roof and all its timbers exists today as a rapidly decaying ruin.

The declining fortunes of the mills on the Mattock and the general trend of depopulation were reflected in the land tenure and economy of the area as a whole. Before the Great Famine, the tithe applotment books of 1835 record that Dowth was a parish divided between 31 landholders who held plots ranging in size from three-quarters of an acre to almost 190 acres and the mean value per acre of the land was £1.74.[37] The typical holding in Dowth in 1835 was 15 acres, five acres less than the typical farm sixty years earlier.[38] This is a reflection of the growing demand for land in the parish in the late eighteenth and early nineteenth centuries, a period in which Irish agriculture was flourishing. More farmers held less than 10 acres than any other range (something which was also true in the 1760s) and over 90 per cent of farms in Dowth parish in 1835 were less than 50 acres in size.

Only two farms, those of Edward Blake of Dowth and Richard Maguire of Newgrange, both cess payers, were over 170 acres. At 190 and 180 acres respectively, these two men had farms more than 280 per cent larger than the next largest local contemporary. Although there were more farms under ten acres than any other size, together these farms occupied a mere 5 per cent of the land whereas Blake's and Maguire's farms put together took up almost half of the land of the parish. This further illustrates the fact that the agricultural and economic life of the parish was dominated by a tiny minority of wealthy gentlemen. Neither Maguire nor Blake owned any of the land within Rossin itself, however, though they would certainly have been involved in local affairs.

Monknewtown parish was tithe free as it had been monastic land in the ownership of Mellifont Abbey so there are no tithe applotment books to allow for a detailed comparison of land tenure with Dowth for 1835. For this, we must await Griffith's Valuation of tenements in the 1850s when the three townlands in and around Rossin (Monknewtown, Balfaddock and Dowth) contained 131 tenements altogether. There were several kinds of holding comprising land-only tenements (27.5 per cent), house-only tenements (26 per cent), and house-and-land tenements which usually came with 'offices' or outbuildings such as barns, stores, piggeries and fowl houses (27.5 per cent). The remaining 19 per cent of tenements were of different kinds and included five caretakers' houses and one herd's house. That there were so many house-only and land-only tenements tells us two things: that there was a high percentage of landless labourers in the Rossin area in the mid-nineteenth century and that there was an equally high percentage of landowners who were either absent or owned several plots of land in the neighbourhood.

In the mid-nineteenth century, half of the farms in the locality were less than 10 acres in size while 90 per cent of farms were less than 100 acres in size. There were 'small farmers' as well, of course, and 15 farms (18 per cent) were between 10 and 20 acres. Nevertheless, the area was still dominated by a tiny minority with two farms of more than 270 acres. Both of these strong farmers lived in Dowth parish – Richard Gradwell, Blake's successor, and Richard Maguire. In 20 years, therefore, nothing had changed. Indeed, the control of the majority of the land by a small minority of individuals was an age-old phenomenon. Gradwell held a total of 326 acres, 314 in fee (or outright) and the remainder from the trustees of the Netterville Charitable

Institution which had been founded by the legacy of the sixth Viscount Netterville in 1826. Richard Maguire leased 275 acres from one George Monsell and occupied the herd's house. These two gentlemen controlled roughly half of the land of Dowth between them or more than 20 per cent of the total area of the three townlands. Neither man sublet his holdings to any great extent which would suggest that both gentlemen used this land as pasture for cattle grazing rather than for tillage which would have dominated the area in the days of the great mills.

Jim Gilligan's *Graziers and grasslands* has already examined the feelings of discontent that cattle breeders brought to rural communities in Meath from the middle of the nineteenth century.[39] In post-Famine decades, cattle stocks all over the country were on the increase. In Dowth, it seems, cattle were replacing people too as between 1841 and 1861, the townland's population fell by over 20 per cent and within a decade it would be halved. The fact that so much of the land around Rossin was being used for pasture by the mid-nineteenth century is a reflection of the hard times which were being felt by the flour mills around the country as a whole in the 1850s. As a result of the shift from arable to pastoral agriculture, the people of Rossin must have shared the hostile sentiments against large cattle dealers which Gilligan described for the Dunshaughlin area. It must certainly have been a staple of conversation in mid-nineteenth-century Mitchell's.

Dowth was subdivided to a much greater extent than the other two townlands. There were 49 land-holding tenants here and the 'typical' farm was just under eight acres in size. The value of land in Dowth had halved between 1835 and 1854 from £1.74 to just £0.91 per acre, a reflection of the reduced demand for land. Monknewtown was divided between only 27 tenants and the typical farm was approximately 30 acres in size, 25 per cent larger than the typical Dowth farm. Nevertheless, farmland in Dowth was still worth a little over 25 per cent more per acre than land in Monknewtown. Monknewtown also seems to have had more of an even distribution of farm sizes with only two farms exceeding 100 acres. Dowth, on the other hand, as we have already seen, exhibited a degree of inequality. Nevertheless, as with Dowth, over a quarter of Monknewtown was held by just two men, James Drew and Archibald Malcolm who both leased their holdings from the earl of Sheffield.

Balfaddock in 1854 was a townland divided between nine landholding tenants who between them held around 326 acres (the same amount which Richard Gradwell alone held in neighbouring Dowth). Two-thirds of farmers in Balfaddock held the normal size tenement for their peers in the area, i.e. farms of less than 10 acres. The three remaining farms were substantially larger: Patrick Drew held two of them, the first of which was just over 73 acres in size and was leased from one James Newman; the second was held from Charles Gradwell and was around 84 acres in size and included a caretaker's house. Drew sublet a small amount of this land as well as several houses which were probably mud-walled labourers' cottages. The remaining and largest farm in Balfaddock was run by Francis Maguire and was also leased from Charles Gradwell. It was 152 acres in size – almost half the area of the entire townland. The average value per acre in Balfaddock was £0.81, roughly in between the other two.

The general picture, therefore, in the Rossin area as a whole is a changing agricultural landscape where land was increasingly dominated by a small number of graziers with the number of cottiers gradually declining. Although it is difficult to assess the true nature of life amongst ordinary people in the area, the faltering population levels give us an indication of their need to find lives for themselves elsewhere. Before the Famine, Dowth had the highest population. In 1841, a total of 339 people lived in the townland of 1,221 acres which translates into a population density of 0.28 people per acre. The people were divided among 57 households which means there were just over 21 acres per household. By 1901, however, there were over 38 acres per household as the population density had fallen to 0.11 people per acre. Similar trends can be seen for the other two townlands.

Because of its abstract nature, the boundaries of Rossin cannot be fixed. They can, however, be approximated from sources such as the grand jury presentment books, parish registers, the Irish Folklore Commission and from personal communication with present-day locals. The extent of Rossin, therefore, has been defined in Figure 2 and in the mid-nineteenth century, this area contained 36 tenements – 16 in Balfaddock, seven in Monknewtown (including the graveyard, school and schoolmaster's house) and 13 in Dowth. A quarter of these were land-only holdings and a quarter were house-only holdings which indicates the concentration of settlement in Rossin and the high number of landless people living there (table 2).

Rossin comprised approximately 85 acres though, as has been pointed out already, this is a largely theoretical figure as the community has no official boundaries. Nevertheless, it is with a reasonable amount of accuracy, based on Griffith's valuation and local information, that we can state that within Rossin there were 24 households in 1854. If we assume that 85 acres is the rough size of the community's living space, we can calculate that there was only 3.5 acres per household at the time which is only 16 per cent of the space available to households in the wider townland of Dowth. By 1901, that figure had only slightly increased to just over four acres since there was only three households less. The population of Rossin at the turn of the twentieth century was 93 which translates to a density of 1.09 people per acre. This, of course, indicates a much more concentrated settlement than the townlands of Dowth, Balfaddock and Monknewtown where there was 0.11, 0.14, 0.10 people per acre respectively. Rossin, despite local depopulation since the Famine, was still a densely populated linear settlement surrounded by largely open fields.

Table 2. Valuation of Rossin tenements, 1854

Townland	Occupier	Immediate Lessor	Description of tenement	Area (acres)	Annual rateable valuation (£) Land	Buildings	Total	Rate per acre
Balfaddock	John Gorman	Charles A. Gradwell	Land	1.91	0.15	0.15		
Balfaddock	Bryan Heaney	Charles A. Gradwell	Land	1.91	0.15		0.15	0.08
Balfaddock	Mary Gogan	Patrick Drew	House	0.00	0.50	0.50		
Balfaddock	Patrick Bourke	Patrick Drew	House	0.00		0.40	0.40	
Balfaddock	Judith Ogle	Patrick Drew	"House, office, garden"	0.38	0.25	0.75	1.00	0.66
Balfaddock	John Gorman	Charles A. Gradwell	"House, offs, land"	3.44	3.10	0.90	4.00	0.90
Balfaddock	Patrick Ginnitty	Patrick Drew	"House, offs, land"	2.77	3.00	0.50	3.50	1.08
Balfaddock	Michael Bryan	Bryan Heaney	House and small garden	0.00		0.25	0.25	
Balfaddock	Bryan Heaney	Charles A. Gradwell	"House, offs, land"	3.56	3.10	0.90	4.00	0.87
Balfaddock	Patrick Berrill	Patrick Drew	"House, offs, land"	4.78	4.50	3.00	7.50	0.94
Balfaddock	John Leech	Judith Ogle	House	0.00		0.25	0.25	
Balfaddock	Patrick Drew	James Newman	Land	73.46	76.00		76.00	1.03
Balfaddock	Rose Mullen	Patrick Drew	House	0.00		0.50	0.50	
Balfaddock	Catherine Roche	Patrick Drew	House	0.00		0.40	0.40	
Balfaddock	Patrick Berrill	Patrick Drew	House and offices	0.00		5.00	5.00	
Balfaddock	Simon Hamill	Patrick Drew	House	0.00		0.40	0.40	
Dowth	Laurence Hoey	George W. Monsell	House	0.00		0.40	0.40	
Dowth	James Stafford	Edmond Wynne	"House, offs, land"	9.71	8.00	0.50	8.50	0.82
Dowth	Michael Elcock	George W. Monsell	Land	13.81	11.00		11.00	0.80
Dowth	Michael Elcock	George W. Monsell	Land	12.06	11.50		11.50	0.95
Dowth	Margaret Smith	Edmond Wynne	"House, offs, land"	12.31	10.85	0.65	11.50	0.88
Dowth	Bryan Heany	Edmond Wynne	Land	17.81	16.00		16.00	0.90
Dowth	John Ogle	Edmond Wynne	"House, offs, land"	34.55	32.00	1.50	33.50	0.93
Dowth	John Gorman	Edmond Wynne	Land	7.86	6.50		6.50	0.83
Dowth	Laurence Hoey	George W. Monsell	Land	4.69	4.60		4.60	0.98
Dowth	Anne Doonen	John Ogle	House	0.00		0.50	0.50	
Dowth	Michael Elcock	George W. Monsell	"House, offs, garden"	0.69	0.50	1.50	2.00	0.72
Dowth	Michael Murphy	John Gorman	House & small garden	0.00		0.50	0.50	
Dowth	Nicholas Smith	Edmond Wynne	"House, offs, land"	3.57	3.00	0.50	3.50	0.84
Monknewtown	Earl of Sheffield	In fee	Land	21.09	13.50		13.50	0.64
Monknewtown		Earl of Sheffield	Graveyard	0.25	0.10		0.10	0.40
Monknewtown	Matthew Smith	John Reynolds	House	0.00		0.40	0.40	
Monknewtown	John Reynolds	Patrick Drew	"House, offs, land"	8.12	8.50	1.00	9.50	1.05
Monknewtown		Earl of Sheffield	School house & master's ho.	0.00		1.50	1.50	
Monknewtown	Richard R. Hill	William Rogers	"House, offs, corn & flour mill, stores, land"	9.39	6.00	134.00	140.00	0.64
Monknewtown		Earl of Sheffield	Roman Catholic Chapel	0.00		10.00	10.00	

Source: Griffith, General valuation of rateable property (pp. 100–1).
Note: all monies have been decimalised for convenience.

There were 76 households in the locality by 1901, the most common family names being Gorman, Drew, Curry and Hoey. The Berrills, Smiths, Ogles and Elcocks who had been living in the area for up to 200 years were fewer in number by the turn of the twentieth century. In Rossin itself, there were approximately 21 households. Table 3 is a list of the heads of these households with their ages and occupations:

Table 3. Heads of Rossin households, 1901

Townland	*Forename*	*Surname*	*Age*	*Occupation*
Dowth	Patrick	Walshe	60	Farmer
Dowth	John	Ogle	46	Farmer
Dowth	Peter	Smith	60	Farmer
Dowth	Daniel	Hoey	50	General Labourer
Dowth	Michael	Smith	55	Agricultural Labourer
Dowth	Mary	Hoey	40	Housekeeper
Balfaddock	Mary	Farrelly	60	Housekeeper
Balfaddock	John	Gerrard	33	Road Contractor
Balfaddock	Patrick	Corrigan	60	Gardener
Balfaddock	Philip	Brien	22	Agricultural Labourer
Balfaddock	John	Ceague	66	Agricultural Labourer
Balfaddock	Robert	Berrill	42	Publican and Grocer
Balfaddock	John	Gorman	51	Farmer
Balfaddock	Patrick	Chevers	48	Farmer
Balfaddock	James	Martin	58	Agricultural Labourer
Monknewtown	Nicholas	Kearney	60	Pensioner, formerly RIC.
Monknewtown	James	McCormick	50	Agricultural Labourer
Monknewtown	Bridget	O'Neill	40	Housekeeper
Monknewtown	Ellen Octavia	Drew	39	Farmer
Monknewtown	John	Gorman	31	Labourer General
Monknewtown	John	Gorman	61	Shepherd

Source: N.A., Census of Ireland 1901, County of Meath, parishes of Monknewtown and Dowth.

Some of these families were well established in the area but almost half of the surnames that had been recorded by Griffith in 1854 were now gone. This implies that although Rossin was still a concentrated settlement, it was fluid in terms of the people who actually lived there. The disappearance of 13 surnames between the time of Griffith and the 1901 Census could be attributed to childless couples and marriage in the case of female residents but emigration was certainly a fact of life for Rossin as can be seen in the Irish Folklore Commission schools' collection. Remembering the former players of the Rossin football team in 1938, several were said to have emigrated to Australia and elsewhere, or to have moved to Drogheda. Since many other players were deceased by the time the essay was written by a young Maggie Marry of Balfaddock, we can assume that the team being recalled was one which would have played against other local teams (like 'Knock-a-Mooneys' of nearby Coalpits townland) around the turn of the century.

An examination of the ages of Rossin residents and of people in the wider community using the 1901 census also reveals the high level of emigration from the area. In the three townlands surrounding Rossin and in Rossin itself, there were many missing from two age ranges in particular: people in their 30s and people in their 50s. Those in their 50s who were missing had probably left during the Great Famine which hit Meath's population hard despite the fertility of the land. Between 1841 and 1851, Meath's population as a whole had dropped by almost 24 per cent and dropped a further 22 per cent during the following decade. The decline did not begin to slow down until the turn of the twentieth century.[40] Those in their 30s would have left more recently in the hope of making new lives for themselves elsewhere. Among them were players on Rossin's football team, frequenters of the public house.

The occupations of those who stayed varied. Naturally, the largest occupation category was agricultural and one third of all the agricultural labourers of the three townlands (i.e. 19 people) lived in Rossin. It is not surprising that a high percentage of those involved in agriculture lived in Rossin since there was such a high concentration of the local population there. In addition, there were six people who gave their occupation as 'farmer' on census night, 1901. As in many other ways already mentioned, Rossin went beyond the typical rural community by also displaying a diversity of occupations outside the agricultural world. There was a retired RIC man living in the caretaker's house of the derelict Rossin Mill and two of his sons were assurance agents. There were also two seamstresses, a carpenter, a coachman, a gardener, a road contractor, a national school teacher and some domestic servants. And of course, there was Robert Berrill, publican and grocer, whose family had lived in the area since the eighteenth century at least and may have been one of Rossin's earliest families. The dispensary which started out supplying basic medical care to the locals under the Poor Law had been succeeded by a shop which relocated itself within Rossin between 1882 and 1909.[41] This is eventually became Smith's and is owned and run today by the descendants of another well-established Rossin family.

There was a range of occupations in Rossin, therefore, outside the confines of agriculture. In addition, there appears to have been a range of experience in terms of wealth and housing during the nineteenth century throughout Rossin and its wider locality. As Geraldine Stout pointed out in her essay, 'the bend of the Boyne', the stratified society of the area is reflected in the housing. Although the majority of landholders in the area were of modest means in terms of the amount of land they held and what it was worth, there were also some very wealthy strong farmers such as Blake, Maguire and Gradwell whose social status during the nineteenth century had been reflected in the official positions they held, for example as members of the Drogheda Union Board of Guardians.[42] These men all lived outside Rossin itself in fine stone houses, the most magnificent being the Georgian mansion, Dowth Hall, built for the sixth Viscount Netterville in the mid-eighteenth century and, by the turn of the twentieth century, home to Robert Gradwell. Married to a French wife, Lady Henrietta-Maria, daughter of an earl, at only 42 years of age Robert Gradwell was not only a substantial landowner but also a major in the militia, a justice of the peace and, therefore, undoubtedly a man of considerable stature in the local community.

Rossin itself never had residents in the same social or financial league as Gradwell of Dowth or even Maguire of Newgrange and in comparison to the wider area, Rossin enjoyed a reasonable level of social equality. There were no great houses on the scale of Dowth Hall or even James Richard Drew's house in Monknewtown. Nevertheless, there were those in Rossin who occupied a middle ground socially, such as the Ogles, Elcocks and Berrills. These families were long-term residents of Rossin itself and were among its most wealthy. The dwellings of these smaller farmers were modest stone houses such as that of John Ogle and the former caretaker's house attached to the mill which was occupied by Kearney, the ex-RIC policeman.

The Ogles were one of only two households in Rossin employing domestic servants at the turn of the twentieth century, the other household being that of Ellen Octavia Drew, a spinster farmer of thirty-nine years who lived with her domestic servant, Jane Keating. The Ogles were one of the oldest Rossin families but were a family in decline by the turn of the twentieth century. In 1854, there had been only two households by that name living in separate townlands the area and by the turn of the twentieth century, there was only one family of the name left in Rossin. John Ogle lived in the southern extremity of Rossin in Dowth townland in in area with a microtoponym of its own – 'Elland' (formerly known as 'Dillon') and their house was known as 'Elland House'. Ogle had five servants and his wife Agnes, who was almost twenty years his junior, did not bear any children. In consequence, the Ogle name had gone from the area by the 1950s. Elland House and the thirty-four acre farm attached to it passed to the McQuillans of Balfaddock and then on to the Cole family from Co. Cavan around 1950. The Ogles are still remembered by locals as one of the last families in Rossin to keep a horse and carriage which they only used on Sundays to go to mass in the chapel. Their servants were required to sweep the lane and road and open the gates in front of them as they went.[43]

Not all members of these middle families were well-off, however, and poorer relations often lived on much smaller plots and in very basic accommodation, such as the many mud-walled cottages, by far the most common dwelling in Rossin and home during the nineteenth century to the labourers who were effectively landless apart from their acre of potato ground. Eight of the 21 (38 per cent) occupied dwellings in Rossin in 1901 were mud-walled cottages with roofs of thatch. Of the 76 households in the three townlands, there were only 18 such dwellings in total which means that 45 per cent of all the mud-walled cottages in the whole locality were concentrated in the 85 acres that made up Rossin (or 3 per cent of the total area of the three townlands). One occupant of such a dwelling in 1901 was 50-year-old Daniel Hoey, a bachelor who worked as a general labourer. He too was remembered by one of the pupils of Rossin National School in the 1930s, Mary Alice Smith (whose sisters, incidentally, continue to run Smith's shop), who wrote:

> There is the ruins of an old house in my home district. Daniel Hoey was the name of the person who lived in that house. There is nothing to be seen of the house now, only some of the walls. The house was thatched and the walls were made of mud. Daniel Hoey lived with himself. He was an old man when he died. He died in hospital. He had two acres of land with the house and my grandmother bought it.[44]

Many of the mud-walled cottages had been replaced before 1900 by the distinctive 'Parnell cottages' following the 1883 Labourers' Act. Those that remained inhabited in the twentieth century have all but disappeared now as many of the families who lived in them were relocated within the locality by the Irish Land Commission. The remains of some of these dwellings can, however, still be seen in the area today, especially along the disused road known as 'Crag Lane' which formed the notional southern boundary of Rossin, connecting the centre of Dowth and the other hamlet of Craud with Dowth Mill. Crag Lane was linked to the Slane–Drogheda road opposite Rossin Mill and would have been important in former times for the transport of grain to the mills. With the demise of the milling industry in post-Famine years, however, it is now visible today over most of its course as merely a set of parallel earthen banks in the fields, a forgotten road leading to forgotten dwellings.

Conclusion: 'Unfinished village'

One of the main objectives of this work was to suggest possible scenarios and timeframes for the emergence of a community which is virtually invisible in the historical record. This may or may not have been accomplished. What is certain, however, is that Rossin is at least a century older than anyone seems to have previously imagined and that its history, directly or indirectly, stretches back hundreds and possibly even thousands of years.

Of the three townlands that meet to form Rossin, Monknewtown appears to be the location for Rossin's 'pre-history'. Although a townland and parish, the actual 'new town' of the monks was located around the medieval church in the northern part of what would be regarded today as Rossin. The 1612 grant which transferred the possessions of Mellifont Abbey to Sir Garret Moore described Monknewtown as a 'town, village and hamlet'. What had begun, therefore, as a monastic farm building or grange had evolved over the centuries into an actual settlement and was a hamlet by the early part of the seventeenth century. As this was in such close proximity to modern Rossin, it is entirely possible that this hamlet was even the forerunner of Rossin itself. All that was required for the settlement to go from being the town and village of Monknewtown to being the Rossin of today was a relocation of less than one hundred metres south to line the Slane–Drogheda mailcoach road at Rossin, 'the little wood', which appears to have mainly comprised undeveloped plots in 1766. This relocation could have begun in the early–mid-eighteenth century under the lease agreements made between Charles Campbell and Charles Caldwell of Newgrange and their tenants, such as Edward Hall, the Berrills and the Smiths who were already being described as 'of Rossen' by that time.

Even the medieval grange of Monknewtown, the possible precursor of Rossin, was itself a continuation or successor of a much earlier settlement. Monknewtown was also known to the Irish-speaking locals of the early seventeenth century as the 'town, village and hamlet of Rathmiskin', a farmstead which in early Christian times (i.e. prior to *c.*1150) would have been a centre of settlement and economic activity and would have fulfilled a similar role as the medieval grange but anything up to a thousand years beforehand. It is not, therefore, beyond the realms of possibility that the Rossin of today is the latest expression of a tradition of settlement in the area which began with an Early Christian ringfort, was superseded by a medieval monastic farm that developed into a hamlet, and ended with the Rossin we know today.

Although we may never know precisely when or how Rossin came into being, it has been shown that people regarded themselves as being from

Rossin as early as 1724, one hundred years before the mill came to command the local landscape. When parents brought their newly-born children to be baptized, they did not give their place of residence as Monknewtown or Dowth or Balfaddock, but as Rossin. This fact alone indicates a sense of community and identity distinct from the wider community of the three official townlands and demonstrates the potential for townland histories to overlook genuine communities such as this one. Unfortunately, it is precisely because the community developed a separate identity to the townlands around that it remains invisible to any local historian who relies on officially-produced material.

Just like Monknewtown in 1612, Rossin was known to the people of the early nineteenth century as a 'village' and was even sometimes referred to as a 'town' by the grand jury. Although these terms were used in the context of their time and more loosely than they would be today, it can be argued that Rossin was well on its way to truly becoming a village in the early nineteenth century and that the only thing which stunted its growth was the Great Famine of 1845–50 and its long-term consequences for Ireland as a whole.

Rossin was set in a prime location with a road and canal network providing efficient communication between the wheat fields and the mills and from these to the market towns and to the wider world through the port of Drogheda. Rossin was also situated on a river, the Mattock, which provided food, water and of course, motive power. In addition to good infrastructure, a successful village settlement needs certain facilities, many of which seem to have been in place in Rossin by the turn of the nineteenth century, including a school, a chapel and even a public house. Rossin Mill, built between 1825 and 1827, was far from being the first of these developments; indeed, it was actually the last of the major structures to arrive in the area. The only item which the mill may actually pre-date in Rossin is Smiths' shop, the forerunner of which was the dispensary marked on the 1882 revision of the Ordnance Survey map on the opposite side of the Balfaddock Road to its present location. All the other facilities, or their forerunners, seem to have been firmly in place before the close of the eighteenth century.

The main thing which Rossin required to make it a village on the same scale as nearby Slane (a classic eighteenth-century planned estate village) would have been a sustainable expanding population. It is difficult to determine accurately population levels for Rossin as it is, afterall, an unofficial place with only metaphysical boundaries but a population of over 200 could easily have been living in the 85 or so acres of Rossin before the Great Famine with the majority of these residing in the linear settlement at Rossin's heart. Had the Famine not struck, Rossin's population would in all likelihood have continued to rise. The infrastructure, the resources, and the facilities were all in place to support a genuine village settlement but the Great Famine brought depopulation and the repeal of Foster's Corn Laws, both of which proved disastrous for the milling industry, for labour-intensive agriculture, and for the community itself. The farmers who had traditionally supplied the mill were forced to grow alternative crops or, more importantly, to turn to pasture which required fewer labourers and, therefore, exacerbated the depopulation trend. The influx of people came to an abrupt halt during the Famine and never recovered, and many of the buildings which made up the original linear settlement of Rossin were abandoned and eventually demolished.

The community did not resume its growth until well into the twentieth century. However, it never at any time lost its proto-village character and this can be seen in the varied occupations of Rossin's residents at the turn of twentieth century. Rather than being a typical rural community, Rossin still had much in common with a small-scale village settlement with dressmakers, photographers, carpenters, assurance agents, schoolteachers, road contractors and retired policemen among its residents. And even though the population of the surrounding area had been decreasing for the previous half century, and even though many of the original families were disappearing, Rossin itself only lost a net total of three households between the time of Richard Griffith in the 1850s and the census at the turn of the twentieth century. The mill was all but gone (apart from its brief reincarnation as a flax mill in the 1930s and 1940s) but the school, the chapel, the public house, and the shop all remained active.

Rossin's development became frozen in time with the Great Famine and even today little has changed since then. The mill and the school may have closed (though the latter continues in use as a function hall) but the other facilities are still in operation. Although many families and members of families have come and gone, many of the locals can still trace their roots back to those mentioned in this work and some to the earliest known residents. Most of the original dwellings have gone but these too are being replaced by the very occasional modern house. The traditional character of Rossin is, therefore, still vibrant, in particular in the public house and in the shop and in the sense of the place as a whole. The ebb and flow of community life continues as it has done since the days of Rathmiskin and the monastic grange.

Notes

ABBREVIATIONS

NA	National Archives
NLI	National Library of Ireland
PRONI	Public Record Office of Northern Ireland
UCD	University College Dublin

INTRODUCTION

1 UCD Ms S. 192, Irish Folklore Commission schools collection (1938), Monknewtown NS.

1. OFFICIAL PLACES

1 J. Brady, 'The kingdom and county of Meath' in *Ríocht na Midhe*, 1, no. 2 (1956) pp 6–7.
2 Ibid., pp 8–9.
3 B. Graham, 'Medieval settlements in county Meath' in *Ríocht na Midhe*, 5, no. 4 (1974) p. 52.
4 Ibid.', p. 53.
5 Fr Colmcille, *The story of Mellifont* (Dublin, 1958), p. 106.
6 NLI, Drogheda Papers, Ms 5880.
7 Ibid.,
8 G. Stout, 'The bend of the Boyne' in FHA, Aalen, K. Whelan, M. Stout (eds.) *Atlas of the Irish rural landscape* (Cork, 1997), p. 306
9 Graham, 'Medieval settlements', pp 42–3.
10 Ibid., p. 41.
11 Ibid., p. 48.
12 Ibid., p. 56.
13 F. Galway, 'Meath tower houses' in *Ríocht na Midhe*, 7, no. 4 (1985–6), p. 58.
14 NLI, Drogheda Papers, Ms 5880.
15 R.C. Simington, *The civil survey, AD 1654–1656, vol. v county of Meath* (Dublin, 1940), pp 351–2.
16 John D'Alton, *The history of Drogheda* (2 vols. Dublin, 1844), ii, p. 432.
17 S. Matthews 'John Boyle O'Reilly – the early years' in *Journal of the Old Drogheda Society*, 11, (1998), p. 45.
18 Geraldine Stout, *The bend of the Boyne* (Dublin, 1997), p. 34.
19 NLI, Drogheda Papers, Ms 5880.
20 Tuck or fulling mills were mills where woollen cloth was continuously beaten until weather proof. See Cyril Ellison, *The waters of the Boyne and Blackwater* (Dublin, 1983), p. 53.
21 C.C. Ellison, 'Bishop Dopping's visitation book 1682–85' in *Ríocht na Midhe*, 5, no. 3 (1973), p. 5.
22 NLI, Drogheda Papers, Ms 5880.
23 *Ordnance Survey field name books of the county of Meath, vol. xxix*. p. 963.
24 NLI, Drogheda Papers, Ms 5880.
25 Stout, *Bend of the Boyne*, pp 41–2.
26 Ibid., p. 42.

2. EMERGENCE OF ROSSIN

1 One of the few writers to go beyond the mill to examine another facet of Rossin is Geraldine Stout who took a part of Rossin to illustrate example of the relationshi between landlords, tenants and subtenants (Stout, 'Th bend of the Boyne', p. 31
2 UCD Ms S. 192, Irish Folklore Commission schools collection (1938), Monknewtown NS.
3 L. Conlon, *The heritage of Collon* (Collon, 1984), p. 2
4 PRONI, D 3541/1/40.
5 I am indebted to Geraldin Stout for bringing this document to my attentior
6 Registry of Deeds, 27194, Book 40, no. 517.
7 NLI, 21 F 78 (63).
8 NA, Ms. 1095/2/50.
9 Stout, 'The bend of the Boyne', p. 310.
10 A.W. Hutton, *Arthur Young tour in Ireland (1776–1779)* (vols. London, 1892), i, p. 4
11 David Dickson, 'Middlem in Thomas Bartlett & D.W Hayton (eds.) *Penal era and golden age* (Belfast, 1979), p 184.
12 Hutton, *Tour in Ireland*, i, p 47.
13 PRONI, T.2965/5, Dr Fos to Sheffield, Nov. 1774.
14 Ibid., /6, J.T. Foster to Sheffield, 6 Dec. 1774.
15 Ibid., /2, John (The Speak Foster to Sheffield, 30 Apr 1774, Sheffield Papers, .
16 Ibid., /8, J.T. Foster to Sheffield, 14 April 1775.
17 Ibid., /19, Dr. Foster to Sheffield, 15 Nov. 1775.

Ibid., /24, Dr. Foster to Sheffield, 19 June 1776.

Ibid., /36, John Foster to Sheffield, 7 Jan. 1777.

Ibid., /109, Foster to Sheffield, 29 March 1794.

N. Fairtclough, 'The end of an era' in *Journal of the Old Drogheda Society*, vii (1990), p. 71.

Ibid., p. 79.

Ibid.

PRONI, D. 207/54/36, Sheffield to Foster, 30 May 1807.

PRONI, T. 2965/173, Foster to Sheffield, 8 Dec. 1799.

Ordnance Survey field name books of the county of Meath, vol. XXIX, p. 354.

Ellison, *The waters of the Boyne and Blackwater*, p. 27.

Samuel Lewis, *A topographical dictionary of Ireland* (3 vols. London, 1837), ii, p. 389.

Hutton, *Tour in Ireland*, i, pp 44–6.

PRONI, D 562/3322, Sheffield to Col. Thomas Foster, 22 Sept. 1809.

NLI, Ms. 4128, No.17, letter from John Foster to William Marshall, 2 Oct. 1819.

NLI, Ms. 9522, Slane mill account book.

NLI, Ms. 9525, Slane mill account book.

Ordnance Survey field name books of the county of Meath, vol. xxix, p. 963.

Mary Cecilia Lyons, *Illustrated encumbered estates, 1850–1905* (Dublin, 1993), p. 168.

PRONI, T.2965/103, Foster to Sheffield, 1 Aug. 1793.

Stout, 'The bend of the Boyne', p. 310.

NLI, Ms. 9526, Slane mill account book.

Thompson, *Statistical survey of county Meath*, p. 49.

John O'Donovan, *Letters containing information relative to the antiquities of the county of Meath collected during the progress of the Ordnance Survey in 1836*. O'Flanagan transcript (Bray, 1928), no. 107.

3. GROWTH AND DECLINE

1 NLI, *Reports on private collections*, No. 390.

2 NLI, Ms. 9522, Slane mill account book.

3 M. Flynn, *Harvest: a history of grain growing, harvesting and milling in Ireland* (Dublin, 1996), pp 2–3

4 Local history notes made by Cyril Ellison, April 1970, held in Meath Co. Library, Navan.

5 O'Donovan, *Ordnance Survey letters*, p. 354.

6 Ordnance Survey six-inch map, county Meath, sheet 19, published 1882.

7 *Drogheda Argus*, 11 May 1861.

8 Information supplied to Mrs Teresa Martin by Fr Callary of Slane.

9 R. Griffith, *General valuation of rateable property in Ireland, counties of Louth and Meath, Union of Drogheda* (Dublin, 1854), pp 100–1.

10 UCD Ms S. 192, Irish Folklore Commission schools collection (1938), Monknewtown NS.

11 NA, Education Files, ED 1/68 No. 5; ED 2/107 folio 13; ED 9/23931.

12 NA, Charitable Donations Index, vol. 3, pp 192–203.

13 *Ordnance Survey Letters*, p. 353.

14 D'Alton, *History of Drogheda*, ii, p. 433.

15 NA, Grand Jury presentment books, 1C.34.136–7.

16 *Drogheda Argus*, 27 July 1861.

17 Ibid., 24 Aug. 1861.

18 Ibid., 23 Nov. 1861.

19 Ibid., 5 Jan. 1861.

20 NA, Census of Ireland 1901, county of Meath, parish of Dowth, no. 6/1.

21 *Minutes of the proceedings of the guardians of the Drogheda union July 1839–March 1843*. Transcribed and Published by St Oliver's Community College, Drogheda, 1995.

22 Flynn, *Harvest*, p. 2.

23 Ibid., p. 91

24 Fairtclough 'End of an era', p. 74.

25 Lyons, *Incumbered estates*, p. xxiii.

26 *Census of Ireland for the year 1851. Part 1. County of Meath* (Dublin, 1852). p. 224.

27 *Drogheda Argus*, 27 July 1861.

28 Ibid., 10 March 1860.

29 Ibid., 17 March 1860.

30 Ibid., 30 March 1861.

31 Ibid., 23 Feb. 1861.

32 Flynn, *Harvest*, p. 99

33 Griffith, *General valuation of rateable property*, pp 100–1

34 Flynn, *Harvest*, p.3

35 Lyons, *Encumbered estates*, p. xxiii.

36 Ibid., p. xxiii.

37 NA, Tithe Applotment Books, 22/48, county of Meath, parish of Dowth.

38 Registry of Deeds, 1095/2/49 & 50., Valuation of tenements.

39 J. Gilligan, *Graziers and grasslands: portrait of a rural Meath community* (Dublin, 1998), pp 48–53.

40 *Census of Ireland for the year 1851*, p. 224.

41 Ordnance Survey map of county Meath six-inch revision (1882), sheet 19, and 25-inch, sheet 19–12, (1911).

42 *Drogheda Argus*, Aug. 1861.

43 Personal communication, Jack Cole, May 2000.

44 UCD Ms S. 192, Irish Folklore Commission schools collection (1938), Monknewtown NS.

Maynooth Studies in Local History

SERIES EDITOR Raymond Gillespie

This is one of six titles to be published in the Maynooth Studies in Local History series in 2002. The first forty titles were published by Irish Academic Press; the next volumes in the series are being published by Four Courts Press. The publication of this series is a reflection of the continued growth of interest in local and regional history within Ireland in recent years. That interest has manifested itself in diverse ways, including new research about the problems of local and regional societies in the past. These short books seek to make a contribution to that research. As in previous years most are drawn from theses completed as part of the MA in local history at NUI Maynooth.

The new studies published this year are concerned, as their predecessors have been, with the problem of how groups of people within relatively well-defined geographical contexts tried to resolve the problems presented by daily life in the past. Sometimes the areas studied may correspond to administrative units, sometimes not. One local society dealt with this year, Rossin, was an 'unofficial place', known as a distinct community only by those who lived there rather than by administrators. Even such unofficial places had problems in daily life. In some cases those problems had dramatic outcomes. Family jealousies over land and marriage could lead to murder. Elsewhere family networks shaped political actions during the land war. Although local historians are fascinated by the unusual and the violent the daily activities of ordinary life are equally important. The commonplace routines of making a living in an industrial town, worshipping at the local holy well in the way determined by local custom or in the parish church surrounded by one's neighbours are part of the story of the evolution of local societies and all are dealt with in this group of studies.

Taken together these new titles demonstrate yet again, if demonstration is still required, the vibrancy and diversity of the local societies which make up Ireland's past. In presenting this diversity to the modern world they also reveal the challenges which await other local historians to take up the stories of their own areas. In doing so they contribute to the lively discipline that local history has become in recent years.